VAPE MANIA

Melvin Provario

VAP☠RACLE

The following is inspired by true events.

VAPE MANIA

A Newbie's Guide to the Evils
of the ELECTRONIC CIGARETTE

Prolegomenon

Every day in America, millions of people are on the verge of buckling to the peer-pressure that demands without reason that they expose their sacred bodies to the evil mind controlling effects of the wicked vapor of the electronic cigarette. The temptation squeezes from all fronts and materializes in all shapes and forms. From the lowlife street vendors peddling their Barney flavored poison in front of preschools and day care centers to the wizards in their high-tech Nicaraguan bunkers stacked with e-cig propaganda data servers cooled via millions of gallons of malarial H_2O, these immoral profiteers are selling the ridiculous and unsubstantiated notion that their "personal vaping devices" (PVs) are a viable cigarette cessation solutions; but what they don't reveal is that huffing liquefied nicotine (referred to by e-cig junkies as "vaping") to replace the leisurely activity of lighting up the occasional square is akin to trying to quit snorting cocaine by smoking crack. Nobody with a face as straight as Zeppo can deny the true nature of what vaping is—freebasing nicotine!

In a modest attempt to implore the most primitive function of the human brain, that of simple common sense, the Institute for the Preservation of the Institution of Cigarettes (IPIC) offers this cautionary tale of one man's downward spiral into the seedy world of vaping. If this volume sways even one lonely, unsuspecting potential victim from making a drastic, irreversible, life changing decision that will result in nothing but woe and desperation, if it stops the mark of one con artist from switching from the socially acceptable habit of consuming a naturally grown plant filtered through health saving cellulose, to hiding behind a urine coated dumpster in an alley in order to suck on a crude contraption made with glowing kanthal and venom soaked silica, powered by a ticking time bomb battery waiting to explode—then IPIC has done its job. After the Wizard of Vape has its caramel flavored curtain pulled away, we hope that the masses will come to recognize that switching from traditional cigarette products to variable voltage death machines is nothing but a shortcut to desolation.

We at IPIC know that the reader may find the following story disjointed and at times borderline incoherent, but we ask that you bear with it and demonstrate a certain degree of patience for the ultimate message it relates, with sympathy for the narrator who wrote this desperate plea for help while under the influence of what is commonly known as e-liquid or e-juice. At one point in time our narrator was scheduled to testify before the Joint Commission for Smoking Out E-Cig Myths, a panel of experts formed as a result of an intensive study conducted by the University of Tucson in Chicago with the cooperation of the United States Postal Service and the Bureau of Alcohol, Tobacco, and Firearms, in order to dispel and debunk the e-cig propaganda; but the commission's star witness, our lost hero Melvin Provario, mysteriously disappeared without a trace before his admonitory words could be enter into the official records.

When IPIC investigated this man's suspicious vanishment, we found his place of residence gutted out by flames. Later we were informed by an anonymous tipster that the contents of a UHoard storage unit registered under Mr. Provario's name was coming up for auction due to non-payment. We were the sole bidder. Inside of it we found a strongbox with the words "They Are a Pack of Filthy Liars" etched into it with a Craftsman brand Phillips screwdriver that was found lodged into the head of a manikin that had a black & white headshot of Herbert Gilbert (who patented a smokeless, non-tobacco cigarette in 1965) Scotch taped to it.

When we opened the box, we were befuddled to find inside of it thousands upon thousands of loose JEB 1.5 rolling papers. Each fragile piece of paper had scrolled on it tiny, barely decipherable words written in pencil by a hand obviously shaky from e-cig addition. Each swatch of paper was photographed and each photo was then pinned to a massive corkboard in a hangar at the Groom Lake Airport in Nevada. What followed was an unprecedented operation that was undertaken by teams of linguistic experts hired by IPIC to arrange each bit of information into chronological order. After painstaking debate, review and editorial by IPIC, finally some light was shed on our victim's seemingly inarticulate gibberish to reveal a true hero's cry for help as his life as he knew it was stripped away from him by the hideous plague infecting our great nation, the electronic cigarette industry.

When presenting this information to a group of senators with the hope that they might help in our campaign to impose a nationwide ban on e-cig products, we were not surprised when we were met with skepticism, for we knew that the e-cig lobby has become a beast that needs to be reckoned with. Some called the following story opportunist bile and still others called it blatant and unforgivable muckraking designed to misrepresent a viable alternative to smoking. We prefer to just call it Melvin.

Due to the nature of the narrator's state of mind at the time of the writing of this memoir and due to the means by which he chose to document his tale of torture, we at IPIC cannot legally call it biography; all we can hope to ask for is that you read the following account of the instances alleged to have occurred with an open mind and decide for yourself. If by doing so, some of those who have already been caught within the tangled web of the e-cig industry's capitalistic infringement upon the traditional tobacco market choose to break loose from the spell and come back to the luxurious world of cigarette smoking, then we at IPIC believe we have done the United States of America a great service.

God Bless America,

Morrison L. Drall, Chairman,
Institute for the Preservation
of the Institution of Cigarettes

PUFF 1

I once stood five feet eight. I was often told that I was handsome in a dark and mysterious sort of way. The feature most often commented on were my brown eyes, described as striking with the ability to petrify and melt simultaneously, especially when I tilted my head slightly forward and looked up under my brooding brows that expressed hard boiled self-preservation with just a touch of sentimentality even when I was doing nothing but lounging back under my fedora enjoying a rich, tasty cigarette. The lines on my forehead were once subtle, although apparently they had the ability to give my thoughts away, and I guess that is what I needed in order to communicate since my lips normally remained just slightly parted, only opening farther to reveal my upper teeth when I had something profound to say without moving the corners of my mouth before taking a slow drag from the cigarette firmly planted between my thumb and three of my fingers.

But as I write this only a few stubborn strands of hair cling to my scalp. I can barely stand and must stoop over like a branch with too many apples on it. My eyeballs protrude like those of a lifeless doll from amidst the filthy flesh clinging to my chiseled skull. My ears have become pink and pointy like those of a pig and my demeanor no longer reflects confidence in myself through cynicism of the world, but instead I stink of fear and untrustworthiness. My precious, snide, purring voice that once seduced damsels in distress with its stern and apathetic tone has become horse and constricted and it hisses as if my tongue is always touching the roof of my mouth. When I speak I make little children run in terror and this for me is what hurts the most, since I am extremely fond of the little tikes.

Yet I have no one to blame but myself for my present state of being. If only I had never put that first electronic cigarette to my lips, I would still be the man that I once was.

I will set out to write one hundred "Puffs". Each Puff will serve as a chapter of my humiliating confession, if not for the benefit of those who may someday stumble upon this memoir then at least for my own peace of mind, to recreate for myself the course of events that led up to my demise so that I may come to an understanding of how I got here.

It all began in Chicago, the city of big smokers, where the taxes collected from the sale of cigarettes help to feed the homeless and maintain public places of leisure sometimes occupied by highly polished stainless steel tributes to the human kidney. Chicago is probably best known for Democratic presidential candidate Morton Downey, Jr.'s short-lived AM-radio talk show, or perhaps for author, illustrator and World War II hero Ernest Beck's "Atlas of Functional Human Anatomy"—but, for me, a citizen of the world who sticks his neck out for nobody, it was simply known as "home".

It was December of 2013, and a brutal winter was upon us. I bummed a Parliament off of Charlie Sheen who was making a scene at a rock club called Tar during a Cyanide Deathsquad concert. I was smoking it outside, along with about three quarters of the audience. It was cold out but we all needed a smoke so there we were due to totalitarian laws spawned by propagandic hysteria. I could hear the music thundering from behind the cinderblock storefront, rattling the little window with the neon Pabst Blue Ribbon sign in it.

I was there with my friend Little Jerry, who recently had a tracheostomy and who was simultaneously sucking on his Carlton and his Pall Mall through the hole in his throat, blowing out clouds of satisfaction from above his Adam's apple. Melany, who I recently had an uninterrupted go at but who was too drunk to remember, had torn the filter off her mysterious, liberating Viceroy so that she could inhale more smoke. She was daintily spitting bits of leaf and paper off the tip of her tongue after every stress soothing pull. Damian, who was Melany's boyfriend but who knew nothing about the night that I had to drag her like a shot deer up her stairs, had recently taken up cigar smoking and was sucking on an ever so classy Montecristo that lit so brightly with every puff that his Javier Bardem nose momentarily glowed Rudolph orange.

"Dog, it's cold out. Phil Robertson is spooning Anderson Cooper, bet," said a hipster whose face looked like Liberace's knuckles.

"I bet the music sounds better inside," said a girl in hole riddled canvas Converse who was hopping up and down in the slush with her hands stuffed in her jeans and a congestion healing, satisfying Newport dangling from her lips.

"What're you some kinda homophobe?" baritoned something slapping a pack of fresh, aromatic Marlboros against the side of its hand.

"Naw dog it's kool," said the hipster as he lit another deeply satisfying Camel with a flared match

13

and a cupped palm.

A group of smokers were discussing what a lucky strike it was that they were able to get their scalped tickets to the concert when I turned to Little Jerry just in time to see him accidentally suck his entire springtime fresh Pall Mall into his throat. It was a freak accident that had nothing to do with the safety of RJ Reynolds' top selling brand. His eyes bulged and he began to wriggle and convulse and bump into people as he struggled to retrieve the cigarette from the depths of his esophagus. The group of smokers asked him to watch what he was doing. "Something's wrong with him!" I insisted but the smokers must have thought he wanted to slam dance to the muffled music because they started pushing him around as he shot sparks out of his neck that floated around like tiny fireflies.

"Little Jerry," I cried, "are you okay?" Little Jerry went spinning around, his hair twirling like the ribbons of a maypole, as he banged his throat with both his fists. He slid between a parked Jaguar® and an Audi RS 5 and he stumbled out onto North Avenue where he was violently struck by a taxi cab. I watched in horror as poor Little Jerry was dragged underneath for half a block while the taxi spouted a gloom of exhaust before his crushed body bounced out from under the rear tires and he rolled to his death, the soggy remnants of his Pall Mall oozing out of his throat.

"Dog, not even," the hipster said as he flicked his butt to the sidewalk.

As Little Jerry was being scraped up and taken away in an ambulance, I looked down at my pack of pleasure inducing Winston in my overcoat pocket, and for some reason (I don't know why) I considered giving up the highly misunderstood tradition of smoking cigarettes.

I went back into Tar and struggled to find my way to the bar through the thick, oily, rancid artificial fog that was blowing off the stage. I waved my arms in front of my face to clear the view and I found the bartender to order a WildFire made with Bacardi 151 and DeKuyper Island Blue, and that's when he appeared—that guy in the checkerboard shirt with the red hair perfectly trimmed around his ear where a gold strawberry glittered on his lobe. He was sitting on a stool, drawing with his lips off a shiny glass tank about the size of a roll of quarters that was connected to a diamond studded canister. Out of his mouth came billowing white fog like his lips were the top of a smokestack spewing into a starry, brisk Sunday morning sky.

"They let you smoke in here?" I shouted over the music.

He took a long drag off of his glittering baton and then he slowly blew two mountainous white clouds out of his nose. "This, mate, is an electronic cigarette," he said, holding it in his fist for me to see.

"Electronic cigarette? How do you light it?" I bemused.

He looked at himself in the mirror that was behind the bar as his thumb pressed a button that lit up at his touch, while digital numbers displayed a countdown within his electronic gadget, and he took another drag. "You don't light it. It's powered by electricity," he said.

I laughed. "A battery powered cigarette? That's the nuttiest thing I've ever heard. So what's making the smoke?"

He took another ten second pull off of it, until the countdown went to zero and the button he was pressing began to blink like a strobe light. "It's not bloody smoke," he said as he exhaled. "It's vapor."

"Vapor?" I asked, dumbfounded.

He turned to me and blew silky steam into my face. It smelled like pineapple and for that brief moment I saw myself on a sunny beach on some tropical island stretched out on a lounge chair under a big palm tree sipping an exotic drink from a straw in a tall glass full of fruit as little girls ran around in their itty bitty bathing suits.

"Triton," the guy said, gripping his e-cig in one hand and offering the other for me to shake.

I took his hand, which felt as light as tissue. "Melvin," I said.

"Google it, Melvin," he said as he winked his lid over one of his bleachy eyes.

"Okay," I said, nodding my head. "Okay, I will. I'll Google it."

PUFF 2

I missed Little Jerry's ceremonial journey into the holy state of ash because I was obliged to play Santa Claus in the Ralph Lauren girl's section at the Megaplex on State Street. It wasn't a bad temp gig. All I had to do was sit on a throne all day wearing a red suit and a beard and let little girls sit on my lap. I had my special touches that made me a good Santa, I think, like sudden thrusts I made with my hips to bounce them up and down and sometimes a gentle massage with one of my hands to a supple young shoulder. I told them they were on my nice list and offered them some candy as well as a kiss whenever I felt it was appropriate.

After work, when I was in the locker room changing my Calvin Klein underwear, I noticed my pack of Winston was empty, so I headed down the street to the tobacco shop, the one that had the wooden Indian in the window holding the sign for the internationally acknowledged Dunhill brand. I was at the glass display counter feigning interest in what was underneath so that I didn't appear too crude when I merely asked for my diurnal pack of squares. The pale lady behind the counter was impatiently waiting for me as she adjusted her wig of long black hair to and fro that was plopped on what seemed to be a bald head. Just then the thought of Triton, the guy from the bar who had the nice red haircut and the checkerboard shirt came to mind, so I asked, "Do you have any electronic cigarettes?"

The woman gasped and planted her fists where her hips should have been. "Nooo," she said as if that should have been obvious.

"Oh? I wonder why not. I hear it's the new Djarum Black," I said, still pretending to look at this or that under the glass.

"Do you know what's in those things?" she asked with hostility in her voice.

"I would imagine tobacco," I said with a shrug.

"No, there's no tobacco in them. It's antifreeze. That's right. Antifreeze! You're smoking antifreeze," she said with a sneer.

"Well there's no need to get dry about it, ma'am," I said, tilting my fedora politely. "I was just asking."

"Those things are made in China you know," she spat.

She was really raising her voice so I looked around to see if anyone else was in the shop witnessing this, when I noticed through the window that the Snake Eyes Convenience Store across the street had a big sign for the Purpo brand e-cig.

"Much obliged," I said and buttoned up my London Fog as I hurriedly exited, making my way under the el tracks across the street. I went into the Snake Eyes and poured myself a cup of coffee so that I wouldn't look like I was too anxious to try the electronic cigarette. When I got to the counter I pretended that I was perusing what was there.

"Is that it?" asked the freckle faced girl working the register.

"What's that?" I asked, pointing to the long slim boxes of Purpo hanging from the wall behind her.

"I dunno," she said.

"Are those electronic cigarettes?" I asked.

"Yeah I guess," she said with a shrug.

"Does that say that each one is equal to two

packs of cigarettes?" I asked with astonishment.

She didn't even bother to look. "Do you want one?" she asked, her gum snapping between her teeth.

"What's in them?" I asked.

"I dunno," she said, "do you want one?"

"Do you have a pineapple flavored one?"

The girl sort of huffed and surrendered and turned around and looked at the packages of Purpo and said, "Uh, I think they come in regular and menthol."

"What does the regular one taste like?" I asked.

"I dunno, just regular I guess."

"Does it taste like tobacco?"

"I dunnoooo," she whined. "Do you want one?"

"Okay, I'll try one, just for the heck of it," I said. "Give me one of the regular ones."

The girl pulled a box of Purpo off the wall and gave it to me. I looked at the package. "It says here it contains 18 milligrams of nicotine. How does that compare to real cigarettes?"

"I dunno," she said and she rang me up and then went on to the next customer as if it was nothing.

I saw a display on the counter with a little pencil tied to a string. "Win a Lifetime Supply of JEB 1.5 Rolling Papers" it tempted, so I filled out the form, tore it off the booklet, folded it up and slipped it into the slot. As I was leaving and I glanced back, I swear I saw the girl behind the counter with her Apple iPhone planted between her shoulder and ear, chewing her gum slowly and staring at me with the most troubling curiosity in her eyes.

Mmmmm....

I got home to my one room studio apartment and boiled a pack of nutritiously inexpensive Maruchan Ramen Noodles that I slurped out of a recycled Dean's French Onion Dip container with crumbled Keebler's Graham Crackers in it, before I sat down near my Dell Latitude D630 Core 2 Duo 2.0GHz 14.1" 80GB XP Pro and peeled the cellophane off the long slim purple box. I opened up the flap and pulled out the electronic cigarette. It looked nothing like Triton's electronic cigarette. In fact, it looked like a real cigarette, although somewhat larger and made out of flexible plastic. I put my lips to the end that had the hole in it and inhaled and there was a light bulb at the other end of it that automatically turned on and lit up purple when I took a puff. I thought there must be something wrong with it because I didn't taste anything, but when I exhaled a cloud of white vapor came rushing out of my mouth like a volcanic eruption.

My eyes rolled up and my head hung limp while drool slowly slimed down onto my lap. A few seconds passed before I snapped out of my state of nicotinic euphoria, at which time I picked my e-cigarette off the floor and took another drag. "Wow!" I shouted and my downstairs neighbor immediately started rapping on her ceiling with the handle of her broom.

Each time I inhaled through my Purpo e-cig, I did so for a longer and longer period of time in order to absorb more and more of the highly addictive phantasm spellbound inside of it, until I could no longer inhale long enough because the purple light bulb would insistently flash after about eight seconds of sucking, momentarily stopping any vapor from coming out, no doubt to tease my craving so that my next puff was all the more eager.

Then out of the blue, I decided to build a house of cards. It was more like a castle, an exact duplicate of the British Royal Pavilion with the Aces of Spades for spires to be exact, in the middle of the room with the five packs I had, as the electronic cigarette dangled from my lips glowing purple with my every manic breath. When I finished my card castle I stood back and took several photos of it with my Vivitar ViviCam and that's when the purple light of my electronic cigarette wouldn't stop flashing. To my dread its blinking battery was already depleted.

I knew there must be something wrong with it since there was no way in god's great shag farm that I consumed the equivalent of two packs of cigarettes in three hours, so I tried whacking it on my desk but that didn't work. I unpeeled the paper that was glued to it, to find inside a transparent plastic cylinder full of wires. I cut it open with an X-Acto knife and I managed to hotwire it to a nine volt battery which gave me a few additional puffs before it popped like a firecracker in my hand, sending plastic shrapnel into my face.

"Stupid Chinese made piece of crap," I cursed and kicked the castle that imploded down to the floor like so many autumn leaves.

I had the most overwhelming craving for nicotine, like no craving I have ever had before, more urgent than an infant's desire for a tit, more unreasonable than a cockroach's need to peruse the wasteland of its splattered friends' corpses as the light goes dim, so I found a cigarette butt in the ashtray and lit it with a Zippo only to discover that it tasted horrible. I coughed like a drunkard waking face first between the legs of a sweaty sumo wrestler, and I rushed to the bathroom where I vomited in the toilet. My graham cracker bile floated at the surface of the water in the form of a skull and crossbones. Yet still I had the craving, so I tried again with another cigarette butt and my reaction was the same.

Something was definitely wrong with me. I couldn't bare the taste of tobacco anymore. Something in the electronic cigarette had hacked into my brain and reprogrammed it so that I could no longer inhale smoke, but would only find satisfaction when I was quenched by a slimy concoction vaporized by electrical wiring.

I grabbed my jacket and rushed out into the night. The local Snake Eyes store was closed for remodeling so I flailed in a panic to gas station after gas station, liquor store after liquor store, sobbing and howling at the moon, until I found a 24-hour Walgreens that would service my needs. The Walgreens didn't carry the Purpo brand but did have the DLite brand, so I bought five of them for $40 and vaped one of them until it was completely depleted on my celebratory walk home. Other pedestrians marveled at the sight of the glowing red tip of the object protruding from my lips as I moonwalked and twirled around on my heels in jubilation, singing to my e-cig, "I couldn't dance for another ah-ah-aha-ah-aha. Aaah-aaaaaaaaah!!".

I spent the rest of the night pacing my room, vaping one DLite after another until finally I collapsed on my futon and passed out, dreaming only of purple and red lights blinking as I walked on clouds that I scooped up with the palms of my hands and ate like cotton candy.

The next day I woke up drenched in sweat. I scrambled on my hands and knees to find the spent e-cigs, desperately attempting to get at least one final puff off each one of their depleted batteries. I barely made it to the Megaplex in time for my stint as the old man from the North Pole because I had to stop at the Snake Eyes to get some more electronic cigarettes that I proceeded to vape in the locker room and in the bathroom and I stealth vaped them under my beard down into the chest of my outfit; and when I had finished bouncing little girls on my lap for the day I went to the ATM and got out as much cash as I could and I bought even more electronic cigarettes, including several Swooshers, the official e-cig of some South Korean woman's basketball team, and a Cad'lack Cartomizer Starter Kit that came with a rechargeable battery, three vaping units and five nicotine cartridges. It all ran me about $200 but it promised to deliver the equivalent of 100 packs of cigarettes, so I figured I should be set for a while.

Little did I know.

To my dismay one electronic cigarette was no longer enough to fix my increasingly intense e-cig withdrawal, so I rigged a Kimberly Clark Surgical Mask with duct tape and poked three holes in it so that I could strap it to my face and insert electronic cigarettes into it, one for my mouth and one for each nostril. It was a marvelous example of ingenuity. I could wear it and inhale the vapor automatically as I went about my daily business such as washing the dishes or reading the latest issue of Seventeen or giving myself a pedicure and then saving the clippings in an Altoids' tin for future use as toothpicks. The drawback to my invention was that when I attempted to exhale through the mask the vapor instead jetted out of my tear ducts, which swelled up like painful red marbles. Also, my face broke out in zits and I developed hideous canker sores and when I took the mask off to eat or drink I had to dig out gobs of menthol flavored gunk from my nose, but nothing could dissuade me from seeking a more intense nicotine rush. Soon my room was littered with spent electronic cigarettes and cartridges, just hollow shells of their former selves.

I duct taped ten e-cigarettes together and attached them to a sub pump and was sucking the vapor through the gritty black hose, when there was a knock on my door. I waved the fog away with my hand and looked through the peephole. It was Damian, standing out there in the hallway with a Cadbury Dairy Milk mustache. "Hold on a second," I said, because I had learned that vapor only lingers in the air for a moment, so I waited until it dissipated before I proceeded.

Damian took a whiff. "What're you doing, making cookies?"

"No, pal, that's the White Fog Bling Minisnap fifty puff sampler," I said.

"Well whatever it is, it's burning my eyes," he complained. "I need to talk to you. Let me buy you some breakfast."

"Now you're talking," I said. "I'll get my coat." I got my London Fog and made sure there was a big fat e-cig in one of the inner pockets and we left down the thin, clunky, bouncy elevator with the accordion door.

We got into his Mitsubishi Lancer Evolution and drove to the YupYup Diner in Wicker Park, where we were seated at a booth. Damian ordered a short stack of whole wheat pancakes with scrambled egg whites and a side of duck bacon and I ordered Jimmy Deans' sausage on a Thomas' English Muffin with Quaker Oatmeal and Grape Smucker's Jelly.

"Melany's pregnant," Damian blurted out as we ate.

"You don't say. Well, congratulations," I said.

"I guess," he said, bowing his head and picking at his egg whites with his fork.

"I take it that it wasn't planned," I said.

"Neither of us can figure it out. We've been very careful. Listen, that night that Melany was hanging out at—"

"Wait, hold that thought," I said and reached into my London Fog and pulled out my e-cigarette. I put it to my lips and sucked on it and it lit up green.

"What're you doing?" Damian asked. "You can't

smoke in here."

"It's not smoke," I huffed. "It's vapor."

A cloud of espresso flavored vapor wafted over Damian's head to a table of senior citizens nearby. "Hey!" an old lady with a four legged walker shouted. "Take that outside."

"It's okay," I said, lovingly sucking on my e-cig. "This isn't a real cigarette." I blew out another cloud toward them that enveloped their table of food like concentrated bug fogger.

"What's your problem?" someone else shouted. "Can't you see the sign?" There was a sign Scotch taped to the cash register with a clipart image of a burning cigarette inside a circle with a slash through it.

"That sign means no smoking. I'm not smoking. I'm vaping." I blew out a cloud of vapor into the face of the waitress as she approached.

"Sir, you can't smoke in here, take it outside."

"I know my rights," I said. "There's no law against vaping indoors."

The short order cook behind the counter said, "Well this isn't smoking either," and he took a sip of water from a glass, held it in his mouth, and then spit it toward me. "That's not illegal either I guess."

"You've been misinformed!" I shouted. "This isn't a health hazard. It's not second hand smoke!" I blew thick vape rings toward a pregnant lady. "See, it isn't going to hurt your baby."

"But it smells like shit!" someone from the other side of the room shouted.

"So ban perfume then!" I shouted back. "Ban B.O.," and I took a big puff and blew out some more vapor. "There's no law that says I can't vape."

"Dude, you're pissing everyone off, chill out," Damian said.

"That's what I'm trying to do," I said, sucking on the e-cig until the light started blinking.

"Well if he gets to smoke in here, then so do I," a biker in a leather jacket and filthy blue jeans at the counter said, pulling out a pack of L&M's.

"Me too," his biker friend said, lighting up a Salem with a Bic and blowing smoke across the faces of the truckers sitting next to him.

A trucker picked up his Early Bird Skillet and mashed it into the biker's face and what ensued was a blur of fists striking flesh and tables over turning and coffee splashing in slow motion droplets from one side of the room to the other and one of the bikers with his cigarette in his mouth was thrown over the counter and landed on the hot grill and he bounced around on it screaming and there was a gunshot and Damian and I dodged through the mayhem on our hands and knees until we slipped out without paying our bill.

"Those guys need a vape," I said.

When we got into Damian's car and I took a vape he told me, "Dude, come on, there's no smoking in my Mitsubishi Lancer Evolution."

"It's not smoking. It's vaping," I insisted.

"I don't care what it is. It's still going to stink up the upholstery."

"I can switch to a pussy flavored one if you like," I suggested.

"Pussy flavored? Does it really taste like pussy?"

"Sort of tastes like Johnson's Baby Powder."

"Dude, I don't care, there's no smo-, uh, whatever you're doing in my car."

"Fine, I'll walk," I said and got out of his car and started walking, sucking on my e-cig as if I was underwater with only a straw for air.

Damian's window came down with a hum. "It's taken control of your mind," he shouted at me. "It's robbing you of your soul."

But I wouldn't listen. All I could do was perform fellatio on my new love, my tubular plastic canister of coffee flavored jism, my love gun ejaculating gaseous nightshade.

Win a carton of cigarettes a day FOR LIFE!!!

Only at participating SNAKE EYES Convenience Stores

Some restriction may apply. Must produce spent cigarette butts periodically to demonstrate that you are smoking in order to continue receiving your carton of cigarettes a day for life. Based on life expectancy the average prize is expected to equal 180 cartons of cigarettes.

With a Stretch Armstrong arm, I reached for the mashed potato ladle but Granmama hissed "You ought to be ashamed of yourself! Shamey shamey shamey." So I pulled my hand back.

My sister Alice sat across from me, with a nicotine patch plastered over the inoculation scar on her forearm, pressing her two hands flat together in front of her face with her eyes closed and her bowtied two young boys, James and Thom, doing the same thing. Granmama's Djibouti friend Boba from the local Snake Eyes was wearing a fez hat, bowing his head as Halo stood back at a distance with one of her teeth sticking out, frantically wagging her rear end with one eye bugging. My brother-in-law Reo sat next to me with an identical nicotine patch peeking out from under his shirt sleeve and his yellow canister of oxygen on the floor next to his chair with the tubes from his nose slung over his left shoulder. And then there was my fat uncle Nick, used car kingpin of the northwest side, patiently waiting to gain another pound, and his wife Virginia, whose sob story was as familiar as a cigar is in Cuba, a blonde haired vixen that couldn't be tamed, a buxom, voluptuous ruby-lipped temptress in silk stockings always sporting a perfect pout. My older brother Corporal Porphy was at the far end of the table in uniform, gesturing with his folded hands for me to do the same. I reluctantly folded my hands together like a pinecone.

"Dear Lord, we thank you for bringing us together for these Thy gifts even though I live right here and these ungrateful children could visit me any time. After all, I did raise them since that half-Irish daughter of mine smoked herself to death may she rest in peace," and Granmama made the sign of the cross, "after that Italian sonofabitch ran off with that Russian bimbo may the star of David crash onto his head if he's not already dead," and she made the sign of the cross again, "and we gather here to celebrate Your birth in the little manger when nobody would give you a home because back in Your day people appreciated a good home and Lord knows my dining room is bigger than this one's entire apartment," and she bowed her head toward me, "and You would think it wouldn't be too much trouble to pick up a phone to see if their poor Granmama isn't stuck in the bathtub since she spent the best years of her life cleaning up after them and making sure they stayed out of trouble when all they wanted to do was smoke like little Humphrey Bogarts. So bless this food that I managed to scrounge up with my pension that I slaved my life away to earn, and that dear, kind Boba helped me to prepare in Thy name," and we all said "Amen" including Boba.

And we were off. We reached for the food like so many Venus flytraps and passed dishes around like a game of hot potatoes as Halo yapped and Granmama hissed, "You're spoiling for it," so I put my glass of cola on the doily. As we ate, Alice asked me how I liked the yams that she made with Jet-Puffed marshmallows.

"I'm having trouble tasting them," I said. "I'm having a serious bout of vape mouth."

"A bout of what?" Corporal Porphy snapped suspiciously.

"It's when your mouth is dehydrated from vaping too much and your tongue feels like a piece of Jack Link's Beef Jerky," I explained.

"How does a vaporizer dehydrate you?" Alice asked.

"You know (wheeze) I hear (wheeze) if you put a pinch (wheeze) of salt in the water," Reo wheezed.

"I want a vaporizer," said James.

"I wanna varipozer too," said Thom.

"Santa's didn't get you guys vaporizers," Alice said, shooing them.

"Here," I said, tossing the boys a box of Machismo Candy Cigarettes that they began to fight over.

"Hey, don't you play Santa?" Uncle Nick asked.

"Not anymore," I said.

"Don't tell me. You got fired again," Corporal Porphy barked and spit some chewing tobacco into a cup next to his plate of food.

"It's seasonal," I said.

"In other words you got fired," he declared.

"It's Christmas, thus there's no more Christmas, thus there's no more Santa," I yelled.

"There's no more Santa?" Thom whined with a candy cigarette dangling from his lips.

"Now see what you've done," shouted Alice.

"Well you could have at least brought the costume for the kids," Uncle Nick said

"Melvin!" Granmama warned. "Stop causing trouble."

"The costume is owned by the company," I said.

"So you can't taste yams?" Virginia asked.

"I can't seem to taste anything. When I first started vaping my taste buds seemed to have come back but now they've completely vanished again."

"Okay, here we go, here we go," Corporal Porphy said, slamming down his fork onto his plate.

"What?" I asked.

"No, by all means, make Christmas dinner all about you. Go right ahead."

"I was just saying," I said and blew my nose into a napkin.

"Oh, Deary, do you have to do that at the table?" Granmama complained.

"Are you okay Mel? You have bags under your eyes," Alice asked

"I can't sleep lately; I have odd vaping dreams that repeat over and over."

"Dry mouth, runny nose, can't sleep. Granmama, he's on drugs," Corpora Porphy said, his absent eyes glittering under his buzz cut.

"I'm not on drugs; in fact I've taken up something that's very healthy. I've been using electronic cigarettes."

"You're using what?" Granmama squealed.

"Electronic cigarettes."

"Oh (wheeze) I hear those things (wheeze) are bad for you," Reo wheezed. "They have (wheeze) lye in them. No wonder (wheeze) you can't taste anything."

"They don't have lye in them," I said.

"Then what's in them?" Corporal Porphy commanded, pointing an atom splitting finger at me.

"Nicotine, among other things. Some ethanol I think."

"Granmama, he's huffing ethanol."

"What's huffing enathol?" Thom asked

"That's when you spray oven cleaner on a rag

and then tie it to you face," Virginia explained.

"Ewwww!"

"It's really not bad. Look—" and I pulled an electronic cigarette out of my shirt pocket and took a drag off it.

"Ooh, look at the pretty light," Virginia mused.

"This thing is saving my life. I haven't had an analog in three weeks."

"A what?" Uncle Nick asked.

"An analog. You know, a *real* cigarette."

"But you said it has nicotine in it," Alice said.

"But it doesn't have the tar or cyanide or any of the other toxins found in cigarettes."

"But it has ethanol in it?" Alice asked.

"And antifreeze and skin moisturizer and flavoring. I don't know what's in the flavoring actually."

"You're smoking skin moisturizer?" Granmama asked.

"It's not called smoking anymore, Granmama. It's called vaping. See," and I took another puff.

"Why does it smell like coconuts?" asked Uncle Nick.

"They come in all sorts of flavors."

"So they're marketing them to kids!" Corporal Morphy accused.

"Does it come in Snickers?" asked James.

"I wanna Sniggers electrocigrett," said Thom.

"You know," Alice said, waving her spoon at me, "that thing is not approved as a smoking cessation device. You're better off using the FDA approved NicoDose with IntelRender® Technology that helps prevent the urge to smoke by delivering therapeutic nicotine through your skin via the patch's specially designed quilted structure. It helps with the side effects of quitting such as irritability, anxiety, difficulty concentrating and restlessness. NicoDose is a proven smoking cessation aid that's even endorsed by IPIC, the Institute for the Preservation of the Institution of Cigarettes."

"Why is it called I-pick?" Boba asked.

"As I said, it stands for the Institute for the Preservation of the Institution of Cigarettes."

"Wouldn't that be I-piss?" Boba asked.

"Why would it be I-piss?" Alice responded nervously.

"Because the C in Cigarette is soft like an S," Boba said.

"I don't know about that, anyway," and Alice spoke very rapidly in a low tone. "Tell your doctor if you're allergic to adhesive tape or if you are taking acetaminophen, caffeine, diuretics, imipramine, insulin, oxazepam, pentazocine, propoxyphene, propranolol, theophylline or vitamins or if you have heart problems, angina, ulcers, high blood pressure, overactive thyroid, pheochromocytoma or skin disorders or if you are pregnant, plan to become pregnant or are breast-feeding." She inhaled and continued. "Side effects include dizziness, headache, nausea, vomiting, diarrhea, severe rash, seizures, abnormal heartbeat and difficulty breathing. If you collapse and you're not breathing while using NicoDose, call your local emergency services at 911. Use only as directed."

"I swear by it," wheezed Reo.

"I actually prefer NicoChicle," said Uncle Nick. "It comes in four sugar-free flavors: Black Ice®, Cinnamon Stick™, Fruity Blunt™ and Mint

Square™."

"So they're marketing them to kids!" Corporal Morphy accused.

"No, because all the flavors taste like complete shit. They come in either 2.5mg or 5mg doses. You can tell which dosage is for you with a simple test," Uncle Nick continued. "If you've never smoked a cigarette in your life and just want to get hooked on NicoChicle, 2.5mg is probably for you. If you've already been diagnosed with at least one health problem associated with smoking, stick with the 5mg dose"

"So you just chew it?" wheezed Reo.

"Right. When you start to feel lightheaded and giddy and you have to take a dump, you stick the gum under your tongue and keep it there until you're jonesing for some more. Then, you chew again and repeat the process until the shit-taste in your mouth is gone and then you pop another piece in. And you can even chew it while you're smoking! Or when you're having sex, right dear?"

"I have a microchip imbedded in my armpit," Virginia said.

Uncle Nick inhaled deeply and then spit out his words all in one breath. "NicoChicle sticks to dentures, dental caps, partial bridges and braces and is considered a choking hazard and also causes hiccups, nausea, sweating, diarrhea, jaw problems and heartburn so talk to your doctor before using NicoChicle if you have a sodium-restricted diet or diabetes and do not take if you suffer from depression as NicoChicle is addictive and causes severe withdrawal symptoms such as nervousness, irritability, dizziness, anxiety, mood changes, trouble sleeping, vomiting, lightheadedness, headache, vivid horrifying dreams, numbness, tingling in hands or feet, swelling, chest pain, confusion, pounding heartbeat, slurred speech, stroke, rash, itching of the mouth, trouble breathing and tobacco cravings so keep chewing NicoChicle at all times." He inhaled desperately, gripping his chest with a clawed hand and barely spewing out, "It doubles your chance of quitting cigarettes when compared to a placebo!!"

"Good God man," Corporal Porhy said, spitting a stream of juicy chewing tobacco into his cup. "Why don't you just *not* smoke?"

"So what do you do with that electronic thingymajig?" Granmama asked. "Do you gradually lower the nicotine dosage?"

"No ma'am, actually I've raised the dosage since I started vaping."

"But how is that helping you to quit smoking?" Granmama asked.

"I've already quit smoking," I explained. "Now, I'm vaping."

"But how do you quit vaping?" Alice insisted.

"You don't," I said.

"You don't?" everyone repeated.

"Let me see that," Granmama said and snatched the electronic cigarette out of my mouth. She put it to her lips and began puffing on it. "Mmmmm. That's not bad."

"Now see what you've gone and done?" Corporal Porhy yelled.

"Can someone please pass the eggplant," Boba interrupted as Halo wagged her rear end and yapped.

PUFF 6

My Swiss cheese heart was a toilet float sunk to the tank of my stomach. I was drained, unmotivated, and it felt like my eyes were looking through my cheeks above the gravest of Leonard Cohen frowns. I couldn't put my finger on why I felt so terrified, so anxious, so sure the phone would ring with bad news. What dreaded repercussions did I anticipate and from what? Did I say something to someone that I knew hurt them deeply inside? Did I need to eat some Skittles? Perhaps some La Fiesta Salted Pumpkin Seeds? The Skittles tasted like soap; the pumpkin seeds made me choke. I could no longer enjoy anything save for the sweet electronic smaze that my lungs absorbed like a Scotch Brite Sponge.

What robotic spider was spinning its web in my chest? What voodoo did the e-cig cast upon me that I would give up a few yards from the goal line with the ball already in my hand? I was wearing my Heisenberg pajamas in public and I didn't know which was worse, that I didn't care or that nobody else did. Maybe it was the fact that I no longer had a job; but no, that wasn't it. I'd find some shitty slacker gig to cover my measly flop house rent. I always did. Maybe it was Melany thinking about me in her subconscious, pregnant, my seed the virus that spawned her cancerous growth, a piss diaper block stacker crayon coloring lunchbox carrying kissing graduating journey to adulthood that I would never say a word to and avoid at all costs. But why now? This wasn't the first time.

I hadn't finished a crossword puzzle in days. All

I could do was fill in the blanks with variations of the word vape: vapitude, vapagory, vapaggedon. I tried to comb my hair but my hands had dumbbells attached to them so I couldn't reach farther than my ears. I even felt sad in the palms of those hands. Maybe I'd be better off if I just walked in front of a taxi cab like Little Jerry did. It was hopeless but I didn't know what "it" was. Was this diarrhea normal? Does anyone else poop like a Dr. Pepper fountain?

Yes, some money would help. Money always helped. Then I'd be able to collect some new brands of e-cigarettes, the only hobby I could find rewarding. Yet the ones I had didn't contain the same punch anymore. I might as well be inhaling water mist. They were tasteless and gave me a migraine and made my teeth hurt and my eyes twitch and they started making me cough and they just seemed like stupid pieces of plastic but I chain vaped them anyway, longing to re-experience that first time when my head hung low and I drooled all over myself.

Had I reached the tipping point? Had I discovered all there was to discover in the world of electronic cigarettes? Did the prospect of never being amazed by a new flavor or enthralled by a new color of blinking light remind me of death? Or did I simply know the truth, that these expensive pieces of plastic were nothing but a lithium battery connected to a piece of wiring that when activated warmed a solution of antifreeze and skin lotion to produce what my body ached for, that the parts themselves were worth mere pennies but nevertheless were putting me in debt.

I couldn't even cry because there was nothing to cry about. My sorrow was just a depleted battery in my throat, sadness for the entire existential concept of existence illustrated by Charles Schultz. Okay, nobody bought me any Christmas presents but I didn't buy anyone any presents so that evened out. Right? Okay, I was living in a single room and couldn't even fart without the downstairs neighbor banging her broom handle on her ceiling but given who I am and what I care about what else did I need? What I needed was for the nausea that wasn't nausea to stop. At least with nausea you can throw up, you can take some Pepto Bismal or drink some Schweppes Ginger Ale or chew on some Wrigley's Doublemint Gum; but this phantom nausea, this sickness that was there but wasn't there, it was torturous, relentless and cruel.

Anyone could say anything to me and I wouldn't debate it. Someone could kick sand in my face and I would just nod. Why did I think I deserved it? What did I do that was so wrong?

I found myself watching James Cagney movies without paying attention to them, just to consume the time, just to get through the hours, just to waste enough of my life until it was time to sleep again with an e-cig in my mouth. Hope was in the mirror, there right before my eyes but trapped behind glass, out of my reach in a reflective dimension that only existed because of my perception. I had nobody to turn to. I couldn't even get enjoyment out of masturbation. Every time I tried to milk it I envisioned it was an e-cig and tried to vape it, injuring my back. When I managed to release it was like blowing my nose. I didn't even bother to throw out the wadded up White Cloud. It cluttered my desk and I knowingly wiped my mouth with it when e-juice sputtered out of my e-cig onto my lips, as if to do something so repulsive that I would tempt my guardian angel to gag so that upon hearing it I would at least be reassured that something else was out there.

Would there never be anything new in my life? Was this it? Waking and mustering enough power to make a can of Progresso Light Beef Pot Roast soup? Shouldn't I have been doing something productive? Passing out Trojans and hypodermic needles in a homeless shelter perhaps? Running into a burning building to save Vapey the Chihuahua and in the process getting third degree burns all over my body so that I could have a change of setting, a hospital room, a change of character, a hero, a change of face, a handsome monster to a repulsive superman? And why did I find porn so gross? I mean, come on. Couldn't I at least find some good porn like they use to make when it played in an actual theater? I know porn actresses aren't supposed to win any Oscars but at least they can act like they're getting laid.

Thank goodness for the hot bath, the makeshift sensory deprivation tank where I could stay for hours and vape away; but like everything else even that turned out to be a lie because the water would turn cold and I'd shrivel into a wrinkled cornichon. I was the blob of slush and salt on the floor oozing out from beneath my boots. I was the only one who knew that everything existed within the Matrix and that made me the loneliest man on what we perceive to be the planet earth. I couldn't taste. I couldn't smell. I couldn't think unless I thought about vaping.

I wanted to hide under the kitchenette sink amongst the long forgotten cans of Raid Max® Bug Barrier and SC Johnson One Step No Buff Wax. There in the dark with my friends the abandoned products, I wanted to slip down into the crevice between the floorboards and cozy up to the decades of dirt. I lined my entire room with transparent plastic tarps, meticulously pinning them to the ceiling with upholstery tacks, and when I was done I stood naked and hummed the theme to Dexter in sobs of surrender until the broom handle started banging. I flicked myself in the eye to see if it hurt and it did. I was in a coffin full of vapor. I called random numbers on the telephone and when anyone answered I shouted "It's not equal to two packs of cigarettes!" and hung up.

I examined my memory bank, traced my entire life, moment by moment, in search of what brought me to this low point, and I found myself coming to a screeching halt on that day in Tar when I stood at the bar. It was Triton's fault. He was the one who exposed me to this devil drug. He was the master of temptation who put this monkey on my back. I suddenly felt a rush of something I hadn't felt in a while. Willpower. I had a purpose. I would seek out this person who hooked me on e-cigs and I would destroy him.

I went searching at night through the cold winter streets of Wicker Park, often grabbing some red haired person's shoulder and yanking him around only to discover the face of a complete stranger. I drew my own artist's rendition of Triton and went to all the clubs that had one-word names, showing it to the bartenders only to be met with rejection and ridicule. One of them even asked if my mommy knew that I was playing with the crayons again. I went to the Fed Ex Kinkos and photocopied the drawing with the word WANTED on it and included my phone number and passed them out to random people on the corner. Then I was bombarded with a series of prank calls.

So I took a job painting children's faces with clown makeup at the Hawk-A-Rama Indoor Flea Market and I forced myself to go through the motions so that I would have a means to continue my search. I placed a personal ad in the free paper requesting Triton meet me at the corner of Milwaukee and Paulina at 5:10 pm sharp and I stood there each and every evening to no avail. I went to the roof of the tallest building and looked down and shouted "Triton!" at each group of people that passed by to see who would look up but everyone looked up and after so many times doing this people started yelling "Triton!" up at me as they passed by. I stenciled "Triton. I'm Coming to Get You" on light posts but someone stole my meme and put it in a text bubble coming out of the mouth of Gary Coleman.

Finally, feeling exhausted and having tried everything I could think of, I sat at my computer and did a search for Triton on Facebook and there he was—the first result. I sent him a private message. "Thanks for destroying my life!" Within moments he wrote back. "Who are you and what are you talking about?"

"I met you at Tar one night. You were at the bar during the Cyanide Deathsquad concert."

"I remember. What's up, mate?" he wrote back.

"I have you to thank for this," I wrote. I attached

44

a photo of my hand holding an electronic cigarette.

"Why are you showing me that cigalike?" he asked.

"You don't remember? You're the one who told me to try this agent of evil."

"Sorry, mate, but I did not tell you to go to the Snake Eyes and get a cigalike. Those things are a rip-off. They're made by Big Tobacco."

"But what you said to me at Tar that night."

"What did I say to you at Tar that night?" he asked.

"You told me, you told me," I thought back to that night, "you told me to Google it."

"And did you?"

"Did I WHAT?????"

"Did you Google it?"

"No."

"So?"

I took the electronic cigarette out of my mouth and looked at it. Now that I thought about it, this wasn't what Triton was vaping. His gadget was made out of glass and was shiny and had a button on it. His gadget had a semi-liquid solution oozing in it as thick as honey. His gadget produced clouds of vapor that he could chase all day.

"Cigalike?" I asked myself. I opened another tab and went to Google and typed in electronic cigarette. The first item that popped up was a website called Vape Mania. I clicked on it and was sent to a forum with thousands upon thousands of pages of in-depth information about advanced vaping products such as tanks and drippers and twisters and mods.

"You fake!" I said to my cigalike and flung it across the room.

I pulled out my wallet and took out my credit card, suddenly feeling healed with a new sense of purpose.

An E-Cigarette Forum Exposed

Deciphering Melvin Provario's encrypted monologue proved to be quite the task indeed, since many of the words scrawled on his collection of cigarette wrappers were transcribed from discussions he had at a website called Vape Mania. We have successfully recreated some of this dialogue in this volume for you, although including all of the text would have proven to be redundant, since most of the conversation repeatedly proved the same point: that the moderators, who oversee the e-cig forums at vape-mania.com, are batshit crazy.

One may assume that the moderators' random acts of sadism against the members of the vaping forum are the result of their own e-juice addiction, that in the time it takes them to wash out their gear, dry burn the wick and refill the tank, their withdrawal symptoms become too overwhelming to bear and they lash out at the very people keeping their forum vibrant. Fortunately this behavior scares many away from the vaping trap before they can get addicted; but for others, those who have decided to self-commit themselves to this online insane asylum that dishes out infractions quicker than a maximum security prison, no abuse from the moderators is enough abuse. However, upon closer analytical observation conducted by psychologists and social media experts commissioned by IPIC, there does seem to be a dubious method to the forum's madness.

This online e-cigarette forum casts its hook into the vast surf of the World Wide Web by floating at the top of the search engines, appearing there as the result of any inquiry conducted about alternative smoking products. Whether you are a newbie searching for a means to have nicotine products illegally delivered to your doorstep via the United States Postal Service or you are a veteran searching for an alternative mesh for your rebuildable bottom feeder, Vape Mania always holds the top ranked spot in the search results. What our computer experts discovered is that there is invisible hypertext embedded within these search results that is constantly pummeling viewers with subliminal messages like a Svengali eye within a spinning serpentine cone. Once you click on a Vape Mania link, the psychological warfare against your common sense and will power is initiated.

In order to participate in the discussions at this particular electronic smoking forum you first have to make a minimum amount of posts in what is called the "Newbie Room". This is a well thought out strategy to weed out anyone who isn't pro-vaping or who might have an opinion that would disrupt the steady flow of income that is generated off banner ads and from their long list of associated vendors and suppliers that are given permission to pitch their products and sell to the forum's unsuspecting victims. It is still unclear exactly what percentage of the profits the forum receives or how much the vendors have to pay for this privilege, but it's safe to say the compensation is undeniably most profitable.

Not all the "newbies" are what they appear to be. The standard newbie greeting goes something like "Newbie from (insert a location) here! Just wanted to say Hi." Often these newbies are just plants from the forum itself to promote certain products. It's not uncommon for a newbie who claims to have just now discovered the forum to then go on about extremely complicated and expensive modified vaping products or to deliver lengthy spiels in praise of a certain brand of e-juice. What we at IPIC wonder is, if the newbie is so new to vaping, how come it has the knowledge of someone who has been vaping for years; and if it has been vaping for years, how come it has never heard of this forum, since Vape Mania controls the flow of information regarding e-cigarettes on the internet? So we are to believe that someone who knows how to build a variable wattage dual coil .5 sub-ohm microcoil attached to the shell of an Atari controller has just now discovered the internet?

If you are foolish enough to register as a member of Vape Mania, at first you will be amazed to find the forum filled with an abundance of information and you may shrug off the constant bombardment by banner ads as a necessary evil, merely a humble means to create income to keep such a gigantic website operational, not ever suspecting that you are subjecting yourself to a masochistic system of abuse and mind control that will eventually turn you into an e-juice zombie, a good little product placement troll repeating the words Vape Mania wants you to repeat, with your freedom of choice stripped from you and your freedom of speech null and void as any prolonged attempt to resist their assimilation will get you banned from the website; and if that happens count your blessings for there is nothing more dangerous in this world than getting between a mafia and its money; so do not be fooled: making tons of money by promoting illegal and unhealthy activity is what Vape Mania is all about.

The e-cig industry is no different than any other drug cartel. Their minions will offer you the first taste for free to get you hooked, but soon you will find that they have stripped you of everything you are worth — your money, yes, but also your dignity and your pride. If you participate in the forum's chat rooms you will be welcomed into a family where everyone does nothing night and day but speak positively about inhaling an unapproved, untested, unregulated vapor into the human lungs, but know that their kindness is but a confidence game working up toward the big score — your soul. Sound like a cult? Well read on.

In reality, the forum is not run by "nice people" and you will discover this soon enough if you dare to question their authority; and believe IPIC, authority they do have. In fact, when it comes to spreading propaganda about electronic cigarettes, they control the sandbox, and that sandbox is populated by a community hell bent on addicting you to the 21st century moonshine called e-juice.

The first thing that you may find suspicious is that their friendly and informed advice and zealous welcomes will appear amongst deleted comment after deleted comment. These are from the silenced ones who are trying to warn you about the conspiracy of this conglomerate, those who have been restricted like prisoners bound in a dungeon with rubber balls shoved in their mouths by moderators who hover over their shoulders, and your shoulder as well, during every moment you spend in the forum, who pry into your thoughts and invade your privacy, who not only moderate but who participate and antagonize in order to test your allegiance.

When you find yourself the victim of the typical sleight of hand scheme from one of their juice vendors, they will take the side of the vendor every time and if you complain, you will be vilified as your value to them begins to wane like sand pouring through an hour glass. They want spenders, not complainers, and in each instance they have devised the perfect response explaining why it is your fault that you are not satisfied: you haven't "steeped" your juice; your taste buds need to heal after years of smoking cigarettes; you need to raise your nicotine dosage; and when all else fails, you're just a newbie who doesn't know what he's talking about (so shut up or you will get banned).

Our undercover IPIC operatives posed as newbies and entered the lair of the dragon and this is what they discovered. There are three tiers of power to the Vape Mania forum. At the top and most visible and trusted is an organization called the Consumer Advocates for Vaping Equality (CAVE). This entity exists as a front for the entire operation, posing as a political group defending your "right" to poison your body by freebasing nicotine. They often fabricate elaborate stories about attempts to ban e-cigs and then when these bans naturally never materialize, they take credit for foiling the plot.

Once you become a member of CAVE, they will have your address and phone number and then it's easy enough for them to check your credit to see what kind of potential mark you are. They will invite you to their website where you will be encouraged to participate in the CAVE forum. However, if you click on their forum link, it does nothing but take you right back to vape-mania.com, where you will be encouraged to buy product after product and where you will be shunned and even ridiculed if you don't. Once in the forum, you will be encouraged to place a banner as your profile signature that declares to the world how many years you had been smoking and how many days it's been since you last had a cigarette, informing the vendors what level of nicotine addict you are, making you easy prey.

The forum has dozens of affiliated vendors who stalk around eavesdropping on the chat rooms, waiting for the right sucker to say the right things. For example, if you mention that your current vaping device isn't working properly, miraculously some stranger will pop into your thread with great news about a half-price sale on some new and more expensive device that is of course nothing more than a cheap hollow flashlight designed to make a piece of wire glow. The actors in this farce often make light of and even brag about suffering from their own addiction, not to nicotine but to shopping for vaping products (laughingly referred to as "shiny new thing syndrome"), posting photos of all their fancy gadgets to prove it. Others will pipe in, encouraging you to join the shopaholics' club, and you may feel like you are part of that family and pull out your credit card and make that purchase in order to bask in the positive reinforcement of congratulation the same way you would at a Disneyland timeshare pitch. After that, these trolls will disappear, never to be seen again on the forum until they pop up for you again under different assumed names when your new device fails to work properly, as it is bound to do.

This bait and switch game may seem bad enough, but when our operatives dug a little deeper, they discovered the bottom tier of the conspiracy, a corporation called Baker Hill Vapor that pumps thousands upon thousands of plastic dropper bottles filled with noxious blends out to the public every day. It seems even the vendors who are there to shill you are being shilled because the main function of Vape Mania is not to give these vendors a steady stream of customers, but to redirect your attention and get you to give your money primarily to Baker Hill. There is one particular thread at the forum about how great Baker Hill is that has remained open and active for years, receiving hundreds of thousands of comments, with comments posted every other minute in the recent activity stream; but when our operatives attempted to start threads with even minor complaints about Baker Hill, the threads were all closed by a moderator within a few hours and comments that explicitly questioned Baker Hill's relationship with the forum were deleted.

This in itself might not be considered pure evil if Baker Hill was indeed supplying top quality e-juice at cut-rate prices as the trolls who spam 24/7 with praise insist they do, but Baker Hill produces nothing but toxic gunk that most likely causes birth defects. You may wonder how this can be, since you researched Baker Hill and found countless video reviews from people testifying to how superior the product is. IPIC operatives discovered that all of these videos have been paid for with bribes from Baker Hill, that each person who posts a positive video review gets a substantial store credit to be used for vaping hardware such as tanks and batteries, so that they can get free stuff as compensation for their fake reviews even if they aren't stupid enough to vape the Baker Hill brand e-juice.

The Baker Hill trolls at Vape Mania are the nastiest of the lot. If you say something that is even slightly short of praise, they will suddenly appear in droves to counter your claims with well-constructed, prewritten statements about how great the juice is; and if you dare to counter them with your own story, with your own opinion, they "report" you to the moderators and you will find yourself banned from the site for a few days, because remember, according to CAVE, Baker Hill isn't trying to sell you overpriced electronics and addictive compounds made in someone's basement—they're trying to save your life!!

As you can see, if you allow yourself to get suckered into the forum's mania you will be left with one choice and one choice only: either play along and promote Baker Hill, or be cut off from the tit that you are sucking on, leaving you alienated and suffering in a perpetual state of cold turkey fever. Once they have you addicted to their e-cigs, they know they have you by the testicles, since the last thing you want to do is cut yourself off from the deathline that is feeding your addiction; so when you witness others getting banned for merely questioning the health and safety of this vulgar behavior, you are in essence being trained to be a good little Vape Mania marionette.

Soon you will be testifying to the entire internet about how healthy vaping is, even though you are well aware that there is no scientific research to back that claim up. The long term consequences of inhaling things that were never meant to be inhaled won't be known for decades, when people start dropping dead with translucent lung disease or going blind from cinnamon poisoning or having vape-babies who come out of the womb screaming for the dripper and a Poldiac mechanical mod with silver plated brass contacts.

Dear Newbie, Vape Mania is not going to bail you out of prison when you are arrested for receiving in the mail prohibited items such as: Class 1 explosive batteries; Class 2 dangerous vapors; Class 3 flammable e-liquids; and Class 6 toxic nicotine concentrates—sent to you in your name in nothing but a plain manila envelope by fly by night companies. Yet that is exactly what Vape Mania encourages you to do, and rewards you for doing, and is fighting for your right to do. Often these illegal items are sent to you across international borders from Chinese sweat shops that make knock-offs and "clones". If you get caught being an accomplice to that, don't be surprised when you are put on the terrorism no-fly list for the rest of your life and don't say IPIC didn't warn you.

One can only speculate how many suicides Vape Mania is responsible for, when lonely, addicted people who are under the impression that their contribution to the forum has been of some value, since they have spent so much time there, made so many friends there, participated in so many seemingly productive discussions, offered so many people so much advice based upon their own field of expertise, whether it be electronics or gastronomy, but who have it all collapse around them when they learn that it was all just pretend play to sell them fifty cents worth of circuits and wires for their entire life's savings. They were under the impression that they were appreciated, that they were part of a cause, that they found a home, so they think nothing of it when they complain to a moderator about the cheap piece of junk that they bought, because they were told the moderators are there to help, to keep the forum free from flamers. But now *they* have been labeled the flamers. In the world of this electronic cigarette forum, a troll isn't someone who causes trouble by being dishonest, a troll is someone who causes trouble by telling the truth — and each instances of so-called "trolling" is worth a two day ban; and complain too much about paying for this and getting that at Vape Mania and you're out of the blue and into the black and once you're gone you can never get back.

In summary, the primary lobbying group for the electronic cigarette industry that is creating the illusion that they are promoting a safer world through untested, unregulated products exists primarily to profit off the industry through banner ads, bullying tactics, bribery and threats, and this entire umbrella of power is controlled by the whim of a handful of batshit crazy moderators.

God Bless America,

Morrison L. Drall, Chairman,
Institute for the Preservation
of the Institution of Cigarettes

I had President's Day off from my temp job breaking icicles off the soffits outside of the windows of elementary schools, so I decided to take some action to protect my rights as DarthVaper, Vape Mania's most eager newbie. I had a copy of the email that I received from the Consumer Advocates for Vaping Equality folded up in my back pocket, which I pulled out and consulted often in my search for the address of the meeting. After crossing an empty lot of February snow and mud, and pacing the block in question several times to the irritation of a guy in a lemon colored Mini Cooper with a stuffed panda attached to its bumper, who was driving around hooting "O-pen Carts!" and handing things out his window to kids wearing skis, I finally decided it must be the loading dock in back of the large appliance warehouse turned art gallery. As I walked up the ramp there were two people standing guard, a guy with huge Bolshevik eyebrows wearing coveralls and puffy black gloves and a woman wearing pantie hose and red high heeled shoes, who had a no-smoking button pinned to the breast of her dress.

"Can we help you officer?" the Bolshevik asked.

I stopped and chuckled, "Do I have the right place?" and I showed them my invitation to the meeting.

"Looks like the NSA is spying on us again," the woman said.

"Where are you hiding your pack of Benson & Hedges, Agent Chesterfield?" the Bolshevik smirked out of the side of his mouth.

"You got me all wrong, pal," I said. "I hate Big Tobacco."

"Isn't it amazing how sugar attracts the antz," the woman nodded.

"Shouldn't you be illegally searching some school lockers somewhere," the Bolshevik asked.

"Look pal, it took forever to find this place. Is this the CAVE meeting or isn't it?"

"Hmm," the guy hummed, "do you think this noob is cool?"

"Let's find out," the woman proposed.

His eyebrows wriggled like two caterpillars as he pulled an oblong purple box out of his pocket and he screwed what looked like a bullet casing to the top of it and he handed it to me, reaching into his other pocket for an amber glass bottle with a black rubber bulb on top.

"What's this?" I asked.

"Let me guess, you vape Purpos," the woman said sarcastically.

"Okay, let me walk you through it," the Bolshevik said condescendingly. "That's a bridgeless atomizer. Open the bottle and then drip three drops into the top of it." I fumbled with the items with my freezing red hands until I managed to unscrew the top of the bottle and I did as instructed. "Now put a drip tip on top," and the woman opened her purse and offered to let me choose from hundreds of little knick knacks. I took one that looked like a kitten with a hole drilled in its head. "Good choice," they both agreed. I attached the kitten to the top of the bullet shell and then put it in my mouth and sucked.

"Press the button," the woman said.

I fiddled around with my thumb until I found

the square metallic button on the box and when I pushed it, the atomizer made a sizzling sound. I sucked through the kitten head and my mouth was filled with the taste of blueberry cotton candy. I exhaled a gargantuan steamy nebula and my jaw dropped as my stomach cramped and I immediately felt like taking a dump.

"Mmmmm. What is it?" I asked.

"Blue Shoe from Vaperella," the woman said.

"It's good," I said.

"Yeah he's cool," she said and proceeded to pull the rolling steel overhead door up like a seasoned OS.

"Let's have my mod back," the Bolshevik said before letting me inside.

I followed a series of arrows drawn on paper with magic marker, down a flight of steel stairs, through a long corridor of doors, across a wide open expanse of hardwood flooring where people were busy setting up an exhibit of what seemed to be ordinary garbage hanging from the ceiling by fish line, through another corridor of doors, down some more stairs, through a storage room of stage props and costumes, into a janitor's closet with a false wall that had been pulled slightly away that I squeezed through, into a manhole down a thick iron ladder and into an unbearably hot boiler room where a group of people were sitting in the steam on folding chairs in a semi-circle around a short angry looking man with a face shaped like lemon, who had huge lips and hairy arms and who seemed disturbed that I was interrupting whatever speech he was making. I whispered an apology as I tiptoed to a table and got a cupcake and a Styrofoam cup of coffee before I pulled up a chair and joined in.

Leaning against the hulking boiler that looked like an ancient freight train with fire roaring behind its grill were a variety of picket signs, poster boards attached to strips of wood. I read them as the furry lemonhead regained his composure:

Vaping Cures Cancer
Breath Vappily, Live Happily
Get Vaporunk but Stay Smober
Vaping Saves Cash so Trash the Ash
Everyone Has a RIGHT to Breath Vapor
My Children Vape Because I Love Them
Suicide Prevention Hotline: 1-800-VAPE
There Are Cooler Ways to DIE Than Smoking
Put Botox Out of Business, Start Vaping Today

Lemonhead gave me a look. "As I was saying, CAVE has been informed by the brother-in-law of the alderman of the fifty-first ward that today the Joint Committee on Finance, Health and Environmental Protection will introduce an up until now secret proposal during a meeting in the City Council Chamber that will ban electronic cigarette products from being vaped on sailboats. We are expecting this to not only involve arrests and imprisonment for anyone caught vaping on personal floatation devices, but it no doubt will also limit the sale of vaping products to land, and even that will be restricted to the cigalikes made by Big Tobacco. Those inferior products will be reclassified as tobacco so that the mayor can line his pockets with new taxes. This proposal is yet another step toward a totalitarian state in which there is door to door searches to confiscate your cartomizers and maybe even your 910 to 510 adapters. Even carrying an ohm chart in your wallet or purse can be probable cause for search and seizure. This new law is a death sentence for vapers who will be forced to fall off the analog wagon. Are we going to allow Big Tobacco to shove their cancer sticks down our throats?"

Everyone shouted "No!"

"Who's the boss of this city?" Lemonhead cheered.

"The taxpayers!"

"And who are the taxpayers?"

"We are!!"

A guy in a flowery shirt raised his hand and said, "I actually live in Florida. Does that matter?"

"I live in New Zealand," a young girl hooted.

"Doesn't matter!" Lemonhead said. "Vapers have to stick together. Let's show those epidermoid carcinoma riddled paper smoking bastards who's the boss!!"

We were all given one of the placards along with a Leonardo DiCaprio mask made out of cheap, brittle plastic that we attached to our faces with a thin rubber band. Once we were all Leonardo DiCaprio we marched in a single file line, chanting "We want an escape! We want to vape!" up the ladder, marching and chanting through the theater storage room and up the stairs, our chants echoing through the art gallery and through the corridors and out onto the loading dock where the Bolshevik and his partner were given Leonardo DiCaprio masks and picket signs and who joined us as we marched through the neighborhood chanting "Get into shape! Start to vape!" and we continued to chant as we marched on the Grand Avenue Bridge over the Chicago River with taxi cabs honking at us and frat boys throwing beer cans at us and pedestrians shrugging their shoulders and we marched and chanted as no doubt swat teams took their positions on the rooftops and helicopters shadowed us from above and we waved our signs above our heads defiantly shouting with a groovy beat through our Leonard DiCaprio masks "You don't get cancer when you vape a Grape! You don't get cancer when you vape a Crepe!" as an army of Chicago police in full riot gear surrounded us and marched with us all the way to LaSalle Street. All the while we puffed on our e-cigs through our Leonardo DiCaprio masks like we were an unstoppable steam engine barreling to its destination, City Hall, where we marched around in circles in front of the entrance chanting "Stop growing tobacco on the roof! Stop growing tobacco on the roof!" until finally a security guard came out of the building and asked what we were doing. "We're protesting the City Council meeting because of the anti-e-cig legislation," we all shouted using various paraphrases.

"There's no city council meeting today," the security guard assured us. "The building is closed. It's Presidents Day." We froze, pondering this, until Lemonhead shouted "We won!!!" and everyone started jumping up and down, cheering and hugging each other.

The next day that was the big news over at Vape Mania, how a small group of protesters shut down a City Council meetings and delayed a vote on the city's e-cigarette ban.

PUFF 8

When I wasn't holding hands with little pigtailed nymphs during my job as a safe-zone crossing guard substitute, I was glued to my Dell Latitude D630 Core 2 Duo 2.0GHz 14.1" 80GB XP Pro, feeding my Vape Mania addiction. Being part of that e-cigarette forum was like taking a masters course in vaping, with interactive classes that ran 24/7, run by strict nuns called moderators who whacked the back of your hand with a ruler anytime you acted up and sometimes just for the heck of it. Putting up with the senile moderators was just the price I had to pay to learn about the vast world of Chinese vaping manufacturers that had new models pumped out as quickly as you could purchase the previous one.

The way the forum worked was that you either started a "thread" or you participated in someone else's thread. You could start a thread merely by making a statement or asking a question. Once you did that others joined into the conversation with comments or answers and you were able to reply back to them, sometimes resulting in a productive focus group and other times resulting in a lively debate if there happened to be disagreements of opinion at which point a moderator would promptly close the thread, restricting it from accepting any more comments, before the civil discourse could turn into an ugly argument.

The rules were very strict. For example, I had recently won a contest and would receive a lifetime supply of JEB 1.5 rolling papers. I was contacted by

UPS and informed that there were several large boxes from JEB waiting to be delivered so I had them sent to my UHoard storage unit. I attempted to post a thread offering to sell some of these cig wrappers at the forum but my thread was immediately closed and I was warned by a moderator that they don't allow solicitation of tobacco paraphernalia and if I continued to break the rules I would face being banned from the site.

Eventually I figured out that you could say just about anything as long as it began or ended with a statement about how absolutely safe it is to vape or how vaping is a miracle drug or how many days I've been analog free or how much money I've saved by not buying cigarettes anymore.

One day I was bewildered to discover the thread I started called "What Kind of Antifreeze Are We Vaping?" had been retitled behind my back to "What Tasty Ingredients Are We Vaping?" I couldn't find a way to fix it. Before that happened I was able to sift through the numerous comments calling me a fear monger and an idiot to discover from someone that the antifreeze used is called propylene glycol, the stuff used as an engine coolant for large tractors, but now that the title had been altered everyone was talking about bubblegum and pomegranate and pie crust.

The lady who lived below me started rapping with her broom handle on her ceiling, making the floor beneath my feet vibrate.

"What's your problem?" I shouted. "I'm not making any noise."

"There's a lady came to my door by mistake, wants to see you!" she shouted up at me.

"Well what the heck are you banging on your ceiling for? Just send her up!"

"She's a real knockout!"

I quickly went to my email inbox to copy the tracking number of the vape mail that I was expecting and I pasted it into the Postal Service's website only to discover its status had not changed from "electronic information received" (same as five minutes before), before I went out into the hall. When the elevator rattled open out walked Virginia, my fat Uncle Nick's wife. She was wearing a green and gold dress with a plunging neckline that glittered like crushed glass over her breasts, her shoulders half covered by a furry stole.

"Well I'll be," I said, tipping my fedora. "Come right in."

"Thank you," she said through her ruby red lips, so softly that I thought there might be someone else behind her. She advanced with hips that could cause a tsunami, looking at me with emerald cat eyes that were both fearful and inviting. Virginia was shaped like a Ming vase from a distance but up close you would need a geometry degree to figure her out. Her legs, like roots hanging out of a flower pot, clacked their high heels like a metronome as her paisley curls of blonde hair brushed my face ever so slightly. She smiled at me with a gap between her front teeth and I could smell her papaya breath as she exhaled nervously.

"Oh, pardon me," I said as I cleared a stack of unopened vape mail envelopes from the chair next to my computer table.

"Thank you," she said as she instinctively minimized the opening of her skin tight dress where one lonely, barely noticeable zit tainted her otherwise perfect complexion. I sank into my clear acrylic low back swivel chair and offered Virginia a polished chrome VAPETekk XMAN with an Id-Tank Cloudomizer attached to it. "No thank you," she whispered, clutching her antique gold stitched leather coach purse.

"Do you mind if I?" I asked.

"No," she shrugged, "go right ahead."

The Cloudomizer was a polycarbonate tube inside a metal covering with a slit in it so that you could see the juice inside, with a clear tip like a plastic vial sticking out of it. I attempted to take a lung hit off of it but it was dry so I took it off the XMAN and turned it upside down and unscrewed its metal base ring and finagled it between my fingers as I went to my shelf that once held books but now held plastic dripper bottles. I chose a lemon meringue pie flavor. Like a person with three hands I managed to squirt some e-liquid into the tank and then reassemble it. I put it back on the XMAN and pressed the button and took a puff, falling back in my chair and moaning with pleasure.

The thing about freebasing nicotine is that the buzz is so temporary that I always snapped out of it within a few seconds with no side effects, except of course for always wanting more. I tracked my package once again and found the status unchanged and then took another vape before I made a quarter-turn to face Virginia with a smile as polite as someone frustrated with the USPS for delaying his nicotine shipment could muster.

Virginia's eyes were uneasy as I blew a cloud. She sat on the very edge of her chair, her feet neatly planted on the floor as if she was about to rise. Her hands pressed down on her dress harder, closing the dark fleshy cavern from my view. I rocked back in my chair and asked, "Now what can I do for you?"

She caught her breath and looked at me, then swallowed and said hurriedly, "Do you-? I heard that—" Then she surrendered and pulled the curls away from her eyes, revealing the tiny strawberry print of her nest. I smiled and turned up the voltage on my XMAN and took a crackling vape but was surprised to find my mouth filled with the taste of burnt rubber.

"Hold on a second," I grimaced and tappity-tap-tapped my keyboard until I got to the proper Vape Mania sub-forum. I typed in "Why does my Cloudorizer taste like a burning tire?" While I was waiting for a reply, I heard a noise and rushed to the window and pulled back the masking tape mended curtain to see if the mailman was making his rounds, but it was only the unfriendly Ukrainian woman who looked like Ronnie Wood walking her two large Finnish Hounds. I thought ahead and connected a charging cable to a different battery and plugged it into the USB port of my computer, when I heard a *bling* indicating I had received a response to my inquiry.

"Did you try taking the flavor wick out?" was the reply, with an instructional video attached to it. I maneuvered my cursor over the play button and tapped my finger on the pointing device and the video started playing. I watched the video twice to make sure I got the hang of it and then took the Cloudomizer apart again, positioning the tank into a pencil holder on my desk so that the juice didn't spill out. I unscrewed the head from the base ring, pulled it apart with a pair of pliers, took off the rubber grommet and gently extracted a tiny piece of silica string from it with a pair of tweezers as I held it under a magnifying lens with a snake light shining on it. I reassembled everything and took a healthy vape.

"Pardon me, you were saying?"

"I don't know where she met him," Virginia cried. "She's as old as blue cheese." Her lips trembled. Her hands mashed her dress back down over her strawberries. "There's nobody I can go to about this, to prove it, you know. But I heard you do temporary work. Is that true?"

"Strictly off the books," I said. As I vaped, the juice began to gurgle and I noticed it was leaking out of the side of my tank. "Hold on," I told Virginia and typed in, "Now it's flooding and leaking." I turned to Virginia and took the opportunity to plant my hand on her knee as I said, "Wait, what are you saying?" and then I heard another noise outside and I spat "Hold on a second," and I went back to the window and saw that the mailman was on the other side of the street making his deliveries. "Oh crap," I said and I rushed to the bathroom to take a dump. I came out wiping my hands on my pants and I heard the computer *bling* so I rushed to it and read the reply: "Did you put the grommet upside down?"

"Ah!" I sighed and took the Cloudomizer apart again, flipped over the rubber grommet and reassembled it. "Are you trying to tell me that you think Uncle Nick's having an affair?" I asked and took a vape but this time juice spit up through the drip tip into my mouth. I gagged and grabbed a

Bounty paper towel and spit into it and then wiped my lips and tongue with it.

"He sits at the computer all night and he won't let me look over his shoulder. But yesterday he forgot to log out and I saw who he's been carrying on with, some old nasty cougar."

"My Cloudomizer is spitting juice," I typed and looked at the clock at the corner of my computer screen. I had been getting vape mail on a daily basis for weeks now and I had the mailman's timing down to an impeccable science. According to my calculations he should be downstairs opening the mail wall in about seven long minutes.

"Try a different mod" was the response.

"What does the mod have to do with the tank spitting?"

"Don't you own a Volarie?"

I rummaged through my unopened vape mail packages until I found the one from Vo-Vape. I ripped it open, retrieving what looked like a fancy flashlight and I frantically slipped in a MNKE 18650 battery and attached the Volarie to my Cloudomizer and tried to take a vape but merely got a mouthful of juice again. "Dammit!" I shouted and typed, "It's still spitting!" I turned to Virginia and said, "You know these variable voltage mods are a joke. You can set them from three to six volts at increments of point one but you can only use them between three point five and four point two. Anything less and there's no vapor. Anything more and it fries your juice. So what's the point?"

"I don't know," Virginia stuttered.

Bling, bling, bling . . .

"The problem is you're using silica wick. Wrap

69

some 32 gauge micron around a 1/16th drill bit ten times and then insert a rolled up piece of sterile cotton ball into it. It'll taste like hydrogen peroxide but meh."

"Easier just to use some cheese cloth."

"I use bamboo yarn. Just boil it for half an hour to wash away any impregnation."

Bling, bling, bling . . .

"bah joos from Baker Hill."

"Why not use stainless steel mesh?"

"Take the tank apart, soak everything in alcohol for a day, dry it and reassembled it."

"What did I ever do to deserve this?" Virginia cried. "He's even starting to smell like moth balls but I don't know, maybe it's just my imagination."

Bling, bling, bling . . .

"Maybe you need to steep your juice. Shake it and then take the cap off and let it sit for three days. If that doesn't work lock it in a drawer for a week."

"Save yourself some time. Boil the bottle of juice for an hour and then shake it and then boil it for another hour."

"bah you joos from Baker Hill."

Bling, bling, bling . . .

"The fastest way to steep is with an ultrasonic cleaner. PM me. I have a coupon code for $150 off. It'll arrive on a slow boat from China but you can't beat the deal."

"I once duct taped my bottle of juice to the blade of a ceiling fan and let it spin for five days. It steeped nicely."

"steep da joos"

"So you don't even know if it's true?" I scolded.

"What?"

"That he's banging some old broad," I snickered.

"I do hope it's not," she whined. "But I need to know—" She broke off with a startled hand to her mouth as I leapt to the window to check on the mailman. I could no longer see him, which meant he was already on my side of the block. Just then the Cloudomizer in my hand made a violent popping sound and cracked in two, the juice sliming all over my palm.

"What the—" I ran to my kitchenette sink and washed my hands before the nicotine could absorb through my skin, then I came back to the computer and typed.

"The tank just cracked in two!"

"What are you vaping?"

"Lemon meringue pie!!"

"The citrus and cinnamon reacted with the polycarbonate. Time to get a new tank. Here's a link!"

"~~Chinese made piece of crap!!!~~" *Comment deleted by moderator.*

The thread was closed and locked after a comment was posted by a moderator: "Try pulling up your big boy pants and stop whining all the time."

"Come on, toots, let's take this downstairs." I grabbed an iShine 45 with a ceramic drip tip rigged with a 1.8 ohm coil, filled with banana cream pie, and screwed it to a TasteRite 3.7 volt battery equipped with a puff counter. I took Virginia by the arm and led her down the hallway to the stairwell which would be quicker than waiting for the elevator. As we stood out front, the mailman slowly going from building to building on his way toward me, I said, "Now what exactly is it that you think I can do about this?"

"I need some proof, one way or the other, of what he's up to."

"Wait, hold that thought," I said as the mailman approached with his cart on wheels.

"Hey Ernesto, como esta?"

"Bueno papa bueno," Ernesto said.

"This is Virginia," I said. "Her husband's dicking some old broad and she wants me to spy on him."

"That true?" Ernesto asked.

Virginia nodded shyly and said something indistinguishable through her pink face.

"That's good," Ernesto said, "that's real good," and he sifted through the letters and packages in his cart.

"What do you have for me today?" I asked, rubbing my hands together.

"Hmmm, don't look like I got nothing for you today papa," Ernesto said.

"What? Are you serious? Look again," I said with astonishment.

"Nope papa don't look like I got nothing for you. Well good luck," he said to Virginia and wheeled his cart inside my building, turning briefly to make a silent whistling shape with his mouth.

"Son of a bridge," I cursed and took a long puff off the iShine.

"What's that you're smoking?" Virginia asked.

"It's supposed to be banana cream pie but it tastes more like a gorilla farted in a bubble bath. It's not too bad. Here, try it," and I gently put the drip tip to Virginia's mouth.

"What do I do?"

"Just suck it, baby, suck it," I said.

I pressed the button on the battery and the juice

inside started sizzling and Virginia's eyes went wide and she mumbled some gibbering as the thick vapor slowly floated out of her nostrils. She moaned and started rubbing her forearms with her hands.

"You like?" I asked.

"I feel strange," she sighed.

"Here. Have another puff," I said and put it to her mouth again. "This time take a slow, long draw, hold it in your mouth for a while to taste the flavor, then suck it into your lungs and then slowly let it slide into your nostrils so that you can enjoy the aroma."

She took a big drag and then coughed it out immediately, swaying on her feet as if she was preparing to collapse.

"What the hell are you smoking over there?" the Neighborhood Watch Commander across the street shouted. "I'll call the cops!"

"This is an e-cigarette, moron!" I shouted back. "There's no law against this."

"Call the cops! Call the cops!"

"We better take this inside," I said to Virginia. "Come on, we'll talk about this over a few vegetable glycerin cocktails.

DarthVaper Out of a whim I ordered some juice from a place called Dracula Vapor. On its way are Vampire Blood™, Spearmint and Berry Cherry. They seemed reasonably priced and had a really good selection of juices. Has anyone else tried this company or these flavors?

Glenn Vampire Blood™ is extremely popular. Be warned not to expose it to sunlight or it will burst into flames lol.

DarthVaper Thanks for the tip. I guess if I'm going to have a new flavor I might as well try the best.

TinyTina Dracula Vapor is not the company known for Vampire Blood. They're cashing in on the extremely popular product made by Dracula Vision.

woodeye Uh-oh. I'll make some popcorn.

smacker I didn't want to be the first to say it.

Elvis the Dracula Vapor one is rank stuff.

mensch Dracula Vision has no pg/vg option but there is at Dracula Vapor

duomas bah joos from Baker Hill

ZestyD Drac Vision is all VG. This is a FACT. Do some research before you say stupid things.

DarthVaper A Dracula war? Wow. Just checked out Vision, doesn't have menthol. Koolada opens up the lungs for better nic-rush.

Moderator There is no discussion of drug use at Vape Mania!!!

DarthVaper ~~I wasn't talking about drugs.~~ *Comment deleted, replaced by Moderator comment:* One point infraction for arguing with moderator.

DarthVaper Oh, ok. LOL. Dracula Vapor has a better variety of flavors like Pizza and Jalapeno with the option of flavor shots and percentage of nicotine.

smacker Vision sells menthol drops separately to add yourself.

DarthVaper Why would I want to do that?

ZestyD Hey newbie get a clue. High end juice makers have menthol just like Baker Hill.

DarthVaper I didn't see that option.

ZestyD Haven't you been listening to FACTS? Dracula Vision has been around for years. They are being ripped off by Dracula Vapor. I can't help the OP if he doesn't want to listen.

DarthVaper ~~There's no need to get hostile.~~ *Comment ruled as "flaming" and deleted by Moderator.*

Elvis I would never trust Drac Vape. When will they run out of ingredients and substitute with bleach?

DarthVaper Here's a link to Dracula Vision Vampire Blood 15ml. I don't see the option to add menthol.

ZestyD Do you have a search box? Use it.

DarthVaper When I Google Vampire Blood, Dracula Vapor is top ranked.

ZestyD I was trying not to flame you for calling me a liar. If you like I will teach you how to use the internet.

JonnyBgood Vision went off-line for months after the hack. I was left jonesing. I hate them. I buy exclusively from Baker Hill now.

DarthVaper When did I call you a liar? It's not my fault Vision isn't promoting itself like Vapor is.

PinchHitter enjoy ur juice scrumbag when it burns a hole in your lungs dont cry to ZestyD who tried to give you FACTS order from Baker Hill next time.

DarthVaper I just wanted some juice. I'm completely neutral about everything. Jeesh.

ZestyD Is this newbie a troll? Vapor is ripping off Vision!!!!! This is a widely known FACT. You are doing business with a known fraud.

DarthVaper ~~I'm not calling you a liar but I'm just hearing about this now and D Vapor is a superior looking company in the variety of juice they offer.~~ *Message ruled "spamming" and deleted, with comment by Moderator posted in its place:* You have already made that point. No spamming.

DarthVaper A company that can't afford to host a proper website is more likely to poison me than a company that can.

ZestyD I spent years looking for the perfect juice and tried hundreds of companies. Short cuts never pay off. Try Baker Hill and you won't need any other company.

StLooey Ripping off a juice is the same as cloning a mod. I'm curious how many kicking up a stink about VB have a K100 or Sigelei or one of those SpeedTekk Generations knock-offs

DarthVaper I didn't take a short cut. I don't care who invented the flavor. I just want some juice.

smacker You put your hand in a hornets nest.

PinchHitter it looks like you want to just argue if that's the case pick something you know what ur taking about. fyi

DarthVaper I'm not arguing. I'm looking for people who have tried Dracula Vapor. Did I mention Dracula Vision?

Toto Isn't the name Dracula copyrighted by Bram Stoker?

PinchHitter trolls will troll

DarthVaper That's what trademarks are for.

Glenn People went into fits when Vision was out of Blood. His store isn't even open during the day. You have to order by night.

ZestyD Everyone here who has ordered fake VB says it tastes like crap. Everyone who buys from Baker Hill has nothing but luv.

ellinoir I hope you have back up heads & some PGA to get the funk out of your clearo dimwit.

PinchHitter curious to see if they refund money when you send it back counterfeit

DarthVaper I'm sorry I even ordered it

chelsie Actual Blood is a complex flavor. It is tough to pinpoint what the flavor profile is.

ZestyD It's just the history of things is all. Order from Baker Hill and you won't be sorry.

DarthVaper ~~Why do you keep bringing up Baker Hill? I'm not even talking about Baker Hill.~~ *Comment ruled "off topic" and deleted, followed by Private Message from Moderator*: You have received an infraction. You are clearly spoiling for a fight. Knock it off!!

Patsy Lol...I fell for it...I googled "vampire blood" last week because I wanted to try it after reading about it and ordered from Dracula Vapor. I'm so stupid. I will have to order the true blood next time or maybe from Baker Hill.

DarthVaper Good grief it doesn't even matter. I got the mint and cherry flavor too you know.

Tortoise ~~I like Alien Vapor's mint. I'll probably order 36 mg with extra flavoring just to use it to mix~~

~~with.~~ *Comment deleted with message from Moderator replacing it:* VM does not allow solicitation from unapproved vendors.

ZestyD The OP has made up his mind based on a website. We may as well be talking to ourselves. Search here at VM first. See what people THINK, learn the FACTS.

DarthVaper I'm here RIGHT NOW searching! Don't insult my intelligence.

HandsumJak Darth, you inadvertently stepped into one of the touchiest subjects around. Folks LOVE them some blood, it is arguably the most iconic and beloved of juices among those in the know. It has a rabid following.

ZestyD Insult your intelligence? Don't assume you have any yet n00b.

DarthVaper Just stop arguing with me, OK?? It's getting tiresome.

Curtis Vaping is still in its infancy. The big boys are not involved. It's a cottage industry not cut throat capitalism.

smacker My uber-nerdness is impressed that someone knew the author of Dracula

donalduk ~~don't get from Baker hill it worse juice in univers~~ *Message ruled as "trolling" and deleted by Moderator.*

theykiltkennah I see it as more of a tribute than a rip-off.

smacker I'm going to bed before this thread gets closed.

ZestyD Puleeeeze...no one is arguing with you so don't say thing that aren't TRUE. Learn the FACTS troll.

DarthVaper Yaaaaaawwwwn

Moderator This thread has run its course...shutting it down.

Private Message from Moderator You have received an infraction. Reason: Multiple identities are against the TOS. Please refrain from creating any others so as not to jeopardize your account here.

PM from DarthVaper I only have one account. I have no idea what you're talking about.

PM from Moderator. You have another username registered as **DunceVaper** using your same avatar making comments in other threads, here are your own comments!! --

DunceVaper "fake Vampire Blood! YUMMY. if sum 1 wants to make busness and joos with same name as establish 1 it aint illegal. if sum 1 set up shop under sum name same as mine thats there right you know?"

And you also wrote the following!!

DunceVaper "sum 1 can start walking round with name like mine and even maybe look like me and I care less. I hate puppies"

PM from DarthVaper WTF?

PM from Moderator That's it. You have been banned from using Vape Mania for two days. Please take this time to rethink your approach.

PUFF 10

I managed to keep my Hawk-A-Rama Indoor Flea Market weekend job until spring. The booth I worked at was sandwiched between a Juggalo piercing salon and a medieval weapons dealer sponsored by the Klu Klux Klan, so I had no problem vaping on the job. I was working at the Tot Mart Toy table that offered free face painting for the kids to attract business, but since there weren't many parents with kids, I usually sat there against the drapery wall and vaped.

Occasionally I would get to perform my duties and if I must say so myself, I was rather good at it. I took special care applying the clown makeup to their delicate cheeks, giving them a temple massage in the process. I paid particular attention to the details of the mouth makeup, ever so slowly and gently rubbing young lips, carefully pinching them between my fingers and pulling them this way and that, accidentally inserting my finger to touch a moist gum or tongue only on the rarest occasion per job. Like a master, I finished the lips by gracefully applying powder with a puff and then gently blowing it off as close as humanly possible by whistling here or there, so precisely that at times my lips would spark a static shock onto her lips, at which point I gave her a nice warm hug and whispered something soothing in her tiny ear. To compensate for the trauma of it, I scrubbed the makeup off her lips with cold cream using the palm of my hand and began again from the rear, going beyond the corner of her lips to the cheek, to create a big joker smile, as I held one of my hands over the child's chest in order to keep her steady and planted my head on her shoulder where I could smell shampoo, as my other hand worked the damp pink flaps of skin that appeared huge so close to my eyes.

I finally broke down to peer-pressure and purchased some juice from Baker Hill. That morning before I went to work, I filled my Hot Pink Anodized Artscraft Locking 510 SkillTank 3 triple bottom coil nicomizer with some Baker Hill sour cream flavor called Albino Eyes and I was eager to try it; but when I took my first vape I was surprised to find it completely vapid. When I blew the vapor out of my mouth an odor saturated the room like a dirtied diaper and everyone around me at the Hawk-A-Rama started frowning. I tried another vape and there was an agonizing pain like a butter knife was poking through my lungs followed by a headache that made my right eye feel like an olive on a toothpick. I lost my equilibrium for a moment and had to hold onto my chair as the room spun.

"Uggh!" I exclaimed. "This is the worst juice ever. This is Baker Hill? It should be called Faker Hill. I'd rather mount a pissed off bucking bronco than vape this Baker crap."

"Mr. Provario, could that be you?" a guy in pink slacks, who was browsing the toys, asked me.

My vision began to come back and I saw one of my former kindergarten students, Francesco Constantine, standing there with a young girl.

"Hey, don't I know you?" I asked the girl.

"I dunno," she said.

"Sure I do. You work at the—"

"What the heck is that? A crackpipe?" Francesco

Constantine asked.

"It's an e-cigarette," I said.

"An e-cigarette?"

"But we in the vaping community prefer to call it a Personal Vaping Device. Hey, long time no see. Are you still at the University of Tucson?"

"This is true. My discipline is organic chemistry."

"That's what I thought," and then the bright idea that would unintentionally change the course of the vaping world forever popped into my head. "Say listen, pal, the juice in this tank tastes like ball sweat. Do you think you can take a look at it and let me know what's in it?"

"I'd need an entire lab to do that, Mr. Provario."

"There's a lab at the university isn't there?"

"I'd really like to help but that would take a lot of work. I'd have to —" and then something popped into Francesco Constantine's head as well. He looked at me as if I had just answered a prayer. "You know, on second thought, let me see that." I gave him my tank and he studied it with eyes on the verge of enlightenment. "This, this," he said, holding it up to the florescent lights and peering through it, "this might not be a bad idea for my senior thesis. A lot of people use these things these days, don't they," he stated.

"Spreading like a case of the clap."

Francesco Constantine seemed to be talking to himself. "But it's not regulated, is it. Hmm. I haven't seen any peer reviewed paper about it. I don't think it's been done yet. Nobody really knows what's in this stuff, do they. Hmm."

"Oh, a little propane-1,2-diol, some glycerol fats and other biodiesel byproducts, natural and artificial flavoring—"

"Okay, Mr. Provario, I'll tell you what, this sounds like a challenge. I'll take a sample and do a chromatographic analysis. Do you have something to put it in?"

"Just unscrew it from the battery," I said.

"You're giving me this," and he looked closely at it to read the writing etched into the stainless steel, "SkillTank 3?"

"I have five more. I'll never be able to get the Baker Hill funk out of that one, not even with an Everclear bath. Hey, maybe it'll inspire you to take up vaping and I'll be the one who saves your life."

"I don't smoke."

"That never stopped anyone from vaping."

Francesco Constantine bounced the tank in his palm and then planted it into his jacket pocket. "Mr. Provario, you might have saved my life after all." He took my number and promised to call me when he got the results. The young girl he was with snapped her gum between her teeth and they were off to see the Juggalo offering to pull out one of his fingernails with a pair of pliers for the highest bidder.

Francesco Constantine happened to call me a few weeks later, on a day when I was already quite frazzled. The day before he called, I was sitting on a bench in the park near the playground having a nice cappuccino vape when I was approached by the cutest woman who I felt an immediate attraction to as if we were soul mates in a previous lifetime. She called herself Yugo. Oh how to describe her. She looked like a young Pia Zadora, with blue eyes that had a bedazzling Nicholle Tom imbalance to them, with puffy Mackenzie Rosman bags beneath that suggested long bouts of reflection and deep underlying wisdom. She was dressed rather plainly in all navy blue, from her knee-high stockings to her plaid pleated skirt to her sweater vest, under which she wore a simple white collared shirt and a matching plaid tie. I could tell from the moment I saw her that she was a being of great intelligence because she was clutching a book on mathematics to her slightly chubby belly area.

"What is that you're smoking, mister?" she asked.

"Starbux. It's imported from China."

"Can I have some?"

"You might enjoy this one better," I said and I searched through my briefcase until I found my Kayjoy 3.1 Hybrid that I had recently spent seven hours rebuilding before filling it with Cookie Monsta juice from Sesame Vape. My Kayjoy was a real beauty, like a silver multilayered wedding cake. I admit I intended to impress by screwing it to a French-made Titanide and offering it to Yugo's mouth like it was the holy sacrament; and I do believe she was making an equal effort by accepting the brown sugary chocolate concoction into her throat without hesitation.

We sat together on the bench for the good part of an hour, laughing and vaping and talking about our plans for the future before I instinctually knew the precise moment to invite her over to my humble abode. There we became cozy on my futon as I taught her how to shotgun vapor from my mouth into hers. Even though she kept telling me she had to leave and even though she asked me to stop, it was crystal clear to both of us that what she really meant was that we were already swept up in the passion of love. There was no keeping us from being absorbed into a moment that would last until the wee hours of the morning.

And it was the wee hours of the morning when things started to get surreal. As the first rays of sunlight broke through the cracks in my curtains, I checked in at Vape Mania to see how many likes I had received for my witty comments, when I saw an announcement concerning a new threat by the evil politicians to ban e-cigs, so I went to an online news site to see if I could find more about it, but instead I saw a blazing headline that read AMBER ALERT with a photo of a child who looked remarkably like my lovely Yugo. When I went to my futon to alert my soon-to-be bride about this coincidence, she was completely unresponsive. I admit what follows may seem a bit rash, but something came over me, an instinctual bout of panic, most likely because I hadn't had my first vape of the day. I searched my vape chest and at first grabbed the spool of Lily Sugar 'n Cream ecru yarn but then decided the 28 gauge heating coil would work better.

Editor's Note: a portion of this memoir has been deemed irrelevant to the discussion at hand — the dangerous properties of electronic cigarettes and the adverse side effects of freebasing nicotine on both the mental and physical health of the victim of this tragic tale; therefore, in order to save space within this book and not distract with off-topic chitter chatter, a chunk of Melvin Provario's narrative has been deleted for your convenience.

I came limping into my room around noon, staggering to the bathroom to rinse the Cuisinart 3-

Speed Hand Mixer under the warm water of the bathtub. My phone was constantly ringing but I ignored it as I used a pair of tweezers to scrape the goop out from under my fingernails. I dumped an entire seven ounce vial of 10% menthol solution into my mouth and forced myself to gargle with it and then I punched the mirror, shattering it, so that I wouldn't have to look at myself, triggering the broom handle below to start rapping. I sat at my desk and had a warm vape to calm myself, took a deep breath, and then picked up the phone.

"Hello, Mr. Provario? It's Francesco Constantine. I have some results for you."

"She should be okay if the wind doesn't blow south," I murmured in delirium

"Listen, besides the antifreeze and skin moisturizer that you mentioned, the sample that you gave me contains 36 milligrams per thousand of nicotine. That's really strong, Mr. Provario, I'd say toxic. It's rather ingenious how whoever made this mixed several food colorings to come up with the milky tint but I don't think inhaling caramel coloring is such a bright idea; it's carcinogenic—and yellow 2 can cause sterility and 5 triggers asthma and red 3 causes thyroid tumors and 40 causes eczema and blue 2 causes brain tumors—"

"She's young. It will grow back."

"Are you with me, Mr. Provario?"

"Sure, pal, I'm listening," I slurred.

"In addition to this, I found ethanol, benzyl cyanide, ammonia, various sulfites and dimethyl amine oxide, none of which are intended to be inhaled. Furthermore, after performing a spectroscopy I found the juice contaminated with traces of iron, chromium and aluminum, most likely produced by the deterioration of the heating element, as well as traces of silica dust emitted from the wicking. Inhaling silica dust damages the lungs, Mr. Provario. You could get bronchitis. In addition there were some other dust sized contaminates that appear to merely be mite feces."

"Wait, what? There's mouse shit in my juice?"

"No, mites, mites."

"Mite shit?"

"Well technically a mite doesn't have an anus. When a mite dies it sort of explodes and releases its entire life's accumulation of feces all at once."

"Mite shit. In my juice? You gotta be floodin' kiddin' me."

"Listen, the mite feces should be the least of your concerns. That's probably just the result of unsanitary lab work. The bottom line is you shouldn't be putting all that other stuff into your lungs."

"Mite shit you say?"

"Listen, Mr. Provario, we're really on to something here. I think I can get a grant for this. In the meantime, I've ordered a bunch of juices from a variety of places. I don't think any of them even have business licenses. I'm just beginning my study on this, Mr. Provario. When I get my paper published we're going to turn the entire industry upside down!"

"Mite shit, eh? Why that ZestyD attyhole! Sure! Buy from Baker Hill, he says." I slammed the phone down and took a pull off my personal vaping device and sat down at my Dell Latitude D630 Core 2 Duo 2.0GHz 14.1" 80GB XP Pro and clicked the Vape Mania bookmark with a vengeance.

DarthVaper I placed an order with Baker Hill and the juice they sent me tastes like poison. I had it analyzed and there's mite shit in it. Why is everyone raving about Baker Hill? It's like the MD 20/20 of e-juice.

Martini Sorry about your luck! I vape BH daily while at work and blast through five tanks. I love dripping my gourmet BH liquids on weekends.

DarthVaper Bad luck?! It has mite shit in it.

Sharkie I ordered 6 flavors and loved it so much I upgraded to 100ml of each...you probably just got a bad batch

Vaporiginal ~~Why does my Baker Hill juice taste like soap?~~ *Comment deleted by moderator, off topic.*

Melvin P ~~Maybe it has soap in it.~~ *Comment deleted by moderator.*

Vaporiginal ~~I only got one juice out of 15 that didn't taste like soap. It all sits in my unvapable closet and has turned black.~~ *Comment deleted by moderator.*

FullGear Baker Hill will give you a $50 store credit for a positive review. You don't get it for negative reviews, Darth.

DarthVaper Sounds skeevy.

Vaporiginal ~~Why were my comments deleted?~~ *Comment deleted, arguing with moderator.*

duomas steep da joos

DarthVaper How is steeping going to get the mite shit out of it?

Penguin You must accept the possibility that you'll have to steep any juice that's mixed to order.

I've found that shaking juice bottles and leaving them sit, uncapped, for two days does the trick. BTW, right now I'm happily vaping Chanel No. 5 from Baker Hill. Can't get enough of this stuff!!

duomas Wah did u have joos analized?

ZestyD There is just so much that is wrong and contradictory with the statements that have been made by this troll who is bashing a respectable company.

ellinoir name one store of any kind that doesn't pay for reviews. its as common as foot fungus. why would anybody fake a good review for $50 credit for a store they don't like?

Private Message sent from DarthVaper Hey ZestyD, thanks for recommending Baker Hill (sarcasm) and stop trying to get my thread closed.

Vapordained ~~I hate BH juice but posted a good review to get $50 for some diy supplies~~ *Comment deleted by moderator, trolling.*

ZestyD Maybe Darth is the problem, not the juice?

smacker Darth, remember when I said I have several bottles still steeping, well, they're STILL steeping. BH reviews remind me of the story of The Emperor...BH is for newbies who don't know what good juice is yet.

ellinoir yap yap only newbies like BH yap yap. the veterans have sophisticated tastes yap yap. yawn.

smacker yawn. Yappity yappity yap.

ellinoir hey now...you started it sport.

LadyV I would like to know what carto, tank or clearo and wattage or voltage the OP is using

DarthVaper What does that have to do with the mite shit?

PM from ZestyD Learn to take advice. Learn the FACTS.

smacker I've received more dud juices from BH than not.

Vaporbiter ~~My only hope is that BH will set the standard for what other vendors will strive not to be.~~ *Comment deleted, flaming.*

LadyV Still want to know what equipment you are using. My BH is vapeable right out the mailbox.

DarthVaper The tank and battery that I'm using have nothing to do with the mite shit

PM from DarthVaper Don't offer me advice if it's going to be in that bullying tone.

LadyV Seriously? I ask you twice simply what are you vaping it in and you can't answer me? This seems very shady. I'm offended that you ignore me, twice!

ZestyD Why isn't the OP answering LadyV's questions? -- devices used, wattage, how or whether you actually steeped the juice, and so on. Context is key.

Vapordiance ~~Bribery is a sha~~dy tactic. ~~Most of us here are addicted to nicotine. $50 of free product would be more than enough to convince a lot of addicts to post positively glowing reviews for a free fix.~~ *Comment deleted, drug talk not allowed.*

ellinoir ~~lol, you make us sound like strung out street junkie crankheads. in reality, i think most of us could scrape together the $50 without having to make a bogus review~~. *Deleted, drug talk.*

Vapordained ~~Don't you work for BH ellinoir??~~ *Deleted, flaming.*

vapity Making a video review is hard work worth more than $50. It isn't worth it.

PM from ZestyD If your thread gets closed it's not because of me, perhaps a good look in the mirror, you started with wanting to have a pissing contest.

Vaporiginal That's not true. You can put your phone in front of your face and talk for a minute and then upload — takes five minutes.

LadyV what clearo, carto you are using, how long the juice has steeped, what voltage or wattage was used, otherwise shut up. OP refused to answer simple questions relating to his own claims.

ZestyD This forum is not for malicious rants by trolls. If someone is going to start a thread here it should be done in a manner that is unbiased and should include facts pertaining to the company or product other than to make inaccurate statements, claims and innuendo. All specifics should be documented as LadyV requested. If there are issues that need to be addressed then those should be included and with what steps were taken to contact the vendor and correct the situation.

DarthVaper What are you, the boss of the thread now?

ZestyD No specifics! No real detail! Never contacted the vendor to correct the issue or get an explanation nor was there any indication that you were interested in having the issue addressed, just the opposite as a matter of fact. This nullifies the credibility of the OP. The Baker Hill customer service is great, but you actually do have to contact them to let them know of a problem.

DarthVaper It has MITE shit in it. How is the vendor going to make that right?

Vaporgasm I havn't found any BH juice that are good right out the mailbox. They all need a good week or two for the flavor to get right

PM from DarthVaper I have no desire to get into a pissing contest with you.

Kango Sounds more like the OP has sour grapes than a real complaint.

ZestyD Agreed, sounds like a hatchet job

PM from ZestyD It's in your nature to have a pissing contest, well perhaps you should stop pissing in the wind! Don't ask for advice if you have no intentions of taking it, the only one you are hurting is yourself!

Secession Preferences in this sphere are profoundly personal and subjective.

DarthVaper Oh shut up!

Secession Did you allow the juice to steep?

duomas wah did u have joos analized

ZestyD The OP obviously has a vendetta

DarthVaper Zesty, I notice you pipe in every time anyone says anything about Baker Hill. Why?

ZestyD I just get irked when someone says false things about a respectable company and doesn't bother to learn the FACTS. Steep it!

DarthVaper For flood sake Irkel, how is steeping it supposed to get the mite shit out of it?

PM from DarthVaper You're really into yourself. Don't impose your issues on me.

Bonzo I diy most of my juices. I always steep them in hot water until it cools. Usually fruits are ready to go almost immediately but more complex stuff tends to mature with age.

TheRightLeft I only steep my juices if I don't like them when I first get them. Some of my subpar flavors have turned vapeable with a couple of weeks cap off aging.

PonchoPilot I put my juice in the clothes drier and tumble it.

Depav ~~BH juice tastes like vinegar and still does after steeping~~ *Deleted, trolling.*

PM from ZestyD You are the one who is too full of yourself. I am not here to argue and I don't have the inclination to play childish games with someone who just wants to create issues instead of taking advice and comprehending what is meant when offering assistance.

DarthVaper I've had enough! I'm going to say it. Steeping is just nonsense. It's a myth invented by subpar vendors who don't want you to return their crappy juices to them. They want you to put it in a drawer for a year instead. Just try returning it to them after a year when it's still no good and see if you get your money back

duomas what u say now bout bh joos?

ZestyD And I've had enough of this troll!! The FACT is that any liquids that are mixed in a complex manner are going to take some aging to meld together, to develop the more complex flavor profiles. The fact also remains that almost all of the flavorings are not completely naturally extracted and are created to mimic the flavor we seek. This is chemistry and rules apply.

PM from DarthVaper You call it giving assistance, I call it bullying

DarthVaper It's not complex at all!! If it's pg and vg and nicotine and cherry flavor—it should taste like cherry not like Pine Sol.

Underdog I have several bottles of BH juice I have been steeping in my attic for the last six months. I can't wait until they are ready to be vaped.

Secession Steeping is yet another part of the trial and error experience that is vaping. You may have to do without some of the higher quality juices like Baker Hill while waiting for them to steep but it's worth it.

DarthVaper Oh shut up already!!!!

PM from ZestyD You just don't want to take things at face value, that's your short comings not mine! Maybe it hasn't occurred to you that those replying to you are actually trying to help steer you in the right direction, instead you turn it into a pissing contest. Take responsibility for your actions, don't blame other for it!

ZestyD Why is this OP still allowed to make comments? I already answered the problem with the FACTS. The real issue isn't mite poop. The FACT is that any complex mixture will require time to develop. I have been dealing with pure essential oils for aroma-therapy, creating lotions and handmade incense for many years.

DarthVaper There aren't any essential oils in e-juice you loonbat!! It's just concentrated flavoring, the same stuff you make Jello or Kool Aid from.

duomas o dah humanity

ZestyD It's a matter of taking responsibility for your OWN actions!!!!!!!

DarthVaper What's that even supposed to mean?? So you're saying it's MY fault there's mite shit in my juice?? Why? Because it didn't sit in a floodin' hole for a month?

ZestyD You are not just letting something sit in a hole, how many times have you, never-mind—

DarthVaper I've never bought a bottle of whiskey and had to age it myself

PM from DarthVaper Baker Hill SUCKS and I know you're just a shill working for them and I'm NOT going to stop saying it just because you bully me like this.

RoseIsRose I really disagree with the steeping thing. I have never in all my years of vaping had a bleh juice turn into a winner no matter how much shaking, hokey pokey, top on off, sitting in a locked chest in a perfectly acclimated room, sticking it in my butt and doing jumping jacks. If it suckath it will always suckath.

DarthVaper Why does nobody seem to care that there is mite shit in BH juice?

PM from ZestyD You are totally unbelievable. I am stating FACTS not trolling threads and making erroneous comments. Stop trolling and you will stop getting called to the carpet for it. If you don't like a company that's fine, stay the hell out of those threads then! Your little attention getting BS is old, grow up!

ellinoir I highly doubt it had mite doo doo in it what does that even mean?

Peepers The aging process allows the propylene glycol and vegetable glycerine to soak up the flavor.

DarthVaper That makes no sense, you aren't drinking it, you're vaping it, it's all getting vaporized together so it doesn't matter how much the flavor is soaked into the other stuff.

Fringe I'm presuming you're a newbie and don't know what you like or what to expect. I highly doubt you got a faulty juice, just one you don't like. If you had been vaping this same juice for a while and got a batch that tasted off, I'd agree that it was faulty.

DarthVaper The only way you would enjoy this CRAP is if you had no nose!!!

wayway BH juice is like a good Cuban Cigar. It starts out 'green' with no complexity. After six months in a humidor it will smell of ammonia. After another 6 to twelve months it's smokeable. After two to three years it's sublime.

Billiards ~~I believe you Darth...that juice probably tastes like ass.~~ *Comment deleted, off topic.*

PM from DarthVaper If you are such an expert then why aren't you getting rich off of it?

Monkeyshine How was the throat hit on the mite shit juice anyway??

duomas jus steep da joos lametard

DarthVaper How did this thread become a conversation about steeping? I just wanted to let everyone know how bad the Baker Hill juice I got is.

Angelina BH prices are great and I always get my orders superfast.

PM from ZestyD Doesn't matter how much money I have. I have over 20 years' experience. You just love to slam a vendor that you personally do not like and your post has no redeemable value. That's trolling!

ZestyD Darth is clearly a TROLL!!!

DarthVaper Stop calling me names!!!! I'm the consumer. I'm PAYING hard earned cash for a product. I expect to be able to use that product without jumping through a bunch of hoops. If the floodin' juice is that complicated that it needs to be steeped, then steep it before you sell it and stop being CHEAP about it.

duomas woh!! wat dis now u say?

PM from DarthVaper I DO NOT want your so-called FACTS attyhole. I've seen you post about how BROKE you are which makes me wonder why such a self-proclaimed EXPERT with so many years of experience can't even make a buck?!!!?

ZestyD It's not a matter of being cheap, it's a matter of giving more choices. If you wish to purchase juice that has been sitting on a shelf for a year, then that's your choice. I like my juices made fresh to order.

DarthVaper Why??!!?? so you can sit it on a shelf for a year??

PM from ZestyD How dare you? You know nothing about me and now you want to get floodin' personal with me.

ZestyD Things are very subjective and not everyone is going to agree. If you wish to be contentious with the recommendations being provided and take them as a personal affront, that is on you. Look for the info and if it's not there move on! Which is what I am now doing from this thread. I'm tired of beating my head against the wall.

DarthVaper I'm tired of every time anyone tries to give their honest opinion about Baker Hill YOU come in the thread within seconds and start bullying people!!!!!!

duomas u are new vape there learning curve u taste buds repairing self u mus lissen to veteran vaper look before you leap.

PM from DarthVaper What are you doing Zesty? Crying like a girl? Ooh poor baby. Don't ever start up with me in a thread again or else.

WillyWonka What duomas means to say is, your taste buds are going to go through some major changes, maybe as long as 8 months after you quit smoking. You're still trying to settle in with a nic level, PG/VG ratio, non-organic or organic, flavor shots, etc. All of those can change the same exact flavor extract into something else. Dead taste buds are not Baker Hill's fault.

DarthVaper blah blah blah

ZestyD If you want to charge into this like a brain dead bull and not LISTEN to the FACTS people are giving you, you're going to make a lot of enemies. This forum is full of people with YEARS of vaping under their belts. Instead of arguing, criticizing or justifying your mistakes and ignorance, EDUCATE yourself.

ropaV I like shiny things

DarthVapor I thought you said you were moving on!!!!!!!

WillyWonka Seriously, dude. Most of your posts are more whining and complaining than anything else.

ZestyD For grommet's sake, put on your Big Boy pants and suck it up.

ellinoir ya suck it up buttercup!

DarthVaper WTF was that?? Triple tagteam match? The juice has mite shit in it.

PM from ZestyD I will post whenever I choose if the information that is provided is incorrect or inflammatory and has no value or basis in fact. And don't make hollow threats, especially ones that you can't back up.

PM from DarthVaper WHAT threat have I ever made. LOL.

PM from ZestyD You make a fool out of yourself every time you post. So give it a rest, grow up and get a life. Not to mention you whine more than anyone else I have ever seen.

PM from DarthVaper You're the one who wants

to get into it. You're the cheap BH-shill.

Juicemeister Darth, you are a noob. Experienced vapers like Zesty are offering up advice so don't knock it. You seem really defensive and I don't know why.

DarthVaper LOL, experienced vapers? You put your lips to it and suck. It's not a game of chess. So do you think when I become a veteran vaper I'm going to want to vape mite shit for some reason???!!!!????

ZestyD As I stated, I am done with this thread. I was actually trying to offer some advice about what I had gone through when I first started vaping. I had to learn on my own and researched and now I make my own juice. As they say "You can lead a horse to a drip tip, but can't make it vape". I don't have the inclination of spitting in the wind in this thread any further.

DarthVaper Do you mean it this time? Will you please leave this time?? This is MY thread!!!

PM from ZestyD You're nothing but a troll. Damn your dumb!

Moderator You ought to be ashamed of yourself. Trolls belong in tree trunks not at Vape Mania. Shamey shamey shamey.

DarthVaper ~~Granmama?~~

Moderator You have been banned from using Vape Mania for life.

DarthVaper ~~Granmama is that you?~~

Moderator Closing thread Deary.

DarthVaper ~~GRANMAMA!!!!!!!!!!!!!!~~

A Brief History of Cigarettes

On the Sixth Day God created Man. On the Seventh Day God rested. When God woke on the Eighth Day he saw what He had done and what He had done was create a living contradiction. The man he created was at once hyperactive while lazy, weight conscience while gluttonous, curious while unfocused, eager to learn while absent minded, on guard but rarely alert, boastful of his manhood while constantly whining about pain, content while troubled with anxiety. This thing called man seemed to live for the sole purpose of fulfilling his sex drive yet was rarely satisfied after having sex. God knew His work was yet to be done. In order to make man whole God would have to create something that was at once a stimulant yet a relaxant, that alerts yet calms, that allows man to feed his pie hole without making him gain weight, that enhances man's memory, reduces his pain and stops his anxiety, and that, most importantly, would give man something to do after having sex. God saw that man had an instinct for survival but nevertheless behaved in reckless ways; so the answer became clear: on the Eighth Day, God created tobacco.

God parted the clouds with his big hands and looked down and spoke, giving life to a potato. God then plucked out one of the potato's eyes and with it He made a red pepper; and the potato and the red pepper had holy copulation, the fat potato just sort of lying there half sunk in the earth sipping on juices and watching the wild kingdom while the thin spicy pepper did all the work, bouncing around above the potato, hanging from the green chandelier of its foliage. Nine months later out popped a little seed from the red pepper, so small a million of them would only weigh three ounces; and in His divine wisdom God planted that little seed in America and it grew into a magnificent tobacco plant to serve as the answer to man's prayers.

You may think this tale is too strange to believe, but scientists and theologians agree — tobacco began growing in the year 6,000 BC, the same year God created the earth.

It took Christopher Columbus 21,000 years to discover America, but when he finally did, what do you think he found? That's right, a bunch of red skinned natives huddled around their teepees smoking American made tobacco in their peace pipes. Few realize that Columbus was a very wise man who intentionally gave the impression that he was a dolt so that he could remain one step ahead of his adversaries. He had a wooden eye that stared straight ahead regardless of what his other eye did and he wore a tattered overcoat and seldom combed his hair. Columbus had an uncanny way of figuring out who did what. One of Columbus' first orders of business was to go on a tour of Kentucky, Tennessee and Virginia where he sampled the fine tobacco products from the friendly natives in their loin clothes and feathery hats, and soon he had them figured out and was smoking with the Indian Chiefs and bartering his pocket watch for a young wife and a bushel of 555 blend.

But there was something missing from the tobacco when it was cleanly smoked out of Indian pipes; and only the white man had the wisdom to figure out how to complete it. What tobacco clearly needed to round out its flavor profile was the scent of burning paper — thus the cigarette was born.

Unfortunately the Native Americans were being rather stingy with their tobacco so God cut them down in size, killing off their buffalo and cursing their blankets and shooting them dead as they rode around in circles on horseback hooting and howling. This opened the door for civilized people to migrate and as they travelled in and out of the promised land they brought their tobacco with them and thus the holy seeds were spread all over South America. Slaves were prohibited to smoke so they hid their cigarettes gripped between their anorecto and since they were often shipped off to Europe to slave for the royal classes, they planted tobacco with their droppings everywhere they went. Nobody quite knows how tobacco made it to the Medieval East but one thing is still clear today, Turkish blends don't hold a candle to what the cowboys smoked to cure bad breath and chewed to ease their toothaches during the birth of this great nation.

By the 17th century tobacco was so popular that it was often used as money. But even back then America wasn't immune to the nonsense of the tree huggers who started making up stories about how addictive tobacco consumption is. Sure it was hard to kick the habit but back then man was still in a Neanderthal state and everything was difficult to quit; heck, robbing banks was difficult to quit. Nevertheless, the liberals of the day often got their whiny little ways and even managed to ban public smoking in Massachusetts.

Up until the year 1760 the cigarette business was just a cottage industry until one day a banker named Pierre Abraham Lorillard was trying to roll his smoke on his front porch in Manhattan, fumbling with it with his clumsy French Protestant fingers, when he saw in the distance a native smoking a pipe, standing beside a hogshead of tobacco, and Pierre had a vision that would transform the image into the best known trademark in the world. That was before his five brothers rushed over and beat the red skinned tobacco thief to death of course. Pierre's wonderful vision could be described with two words: Big Tobacco.

When the trial-lawyer loving Frappucino sipping twits heard about Big Tobacco they went on a sixteen year slander campaign against cigarettes, sending poor Lorillard to an early grave. They didn't have the internet back then, so rumors flew and people started blaming the Brits for poor Pierre's demise and this sparked the revolutionary war. Like the two-faced weasel wafflers they still are today, the liberals had no complaints when this great nation was forced to use tobacco as collateral to borrow loans from the French in order to finance and win the war. So the next time you hang your flag, thank Big Tobacco for your freedom.

In 1828 something would happen that was a liberal's wet dream. Some Nazi over in Germany managed to isolate the nicotine from the tobacco plant and it was discovered that in its concentrated form, it was a poison. Without even bothering to learn the FACTS, about the story of a humble Portuguese colonist in São Paulo named Luis de Gois, who had his Brazilian tobacco stolen by a

French ambassador named Nicot, who then took credit for its discovery, named the active ingredient in it after himself and sold it out of the side of a wagon in Paris as Nicotina, the cure all elixir — nicotine was labeled by the liberals as a deadly pesticide.

The world kept on spinning, so the tables turned in 1849, when J.E. Liggett and his brothers jumped onto the Big Tobacco bandwagon. A profitable new market for them appeared after the North won a four year war and slaves were given the right to smoke. In 1875, the RJ Reynolds Company was going broke supplying cigarettes to its aluminum foundry workers, so it decided it would be cheaper to simply make its own cigarettes and to sell whatever scraps were left to the general public. There was no stopping Big Tobacco with these giants on the playing field. By 1901, three and a half billion cigarettes a year were being sold and in 1902 the first mass marketing of this God given product materialized when the Brits set up Phillip Morris in New York to promote Marlboro.

Everyone was enjoying a good smoke! But the giants were growing faster than the demand, so they had to open up new markets. In 1913, Big Tobacco invented the "soldier's smoke" but soon learned the "soldier's market" was still rather slim with no major wars going on, so they conducted a focus group and came up with a solution. In 1914 a psychopathic Bosnian convict named Gavrilo Princip was hired to assassinate Austrian Archduke Franz Ferdinand in hopes of starting a small confrontation that would create a demand for soldiers. This marketing strategy succeeded beyond anyone's wildest expectations, when on June 28th of that year Gavrilo hacked the poor schlob into tiny pieces with a sickle and when Mrs. Ferdinand came home unexpectedly, Gavrilo raped her on the royal rug, bashed her head in with a statue of Franz Joseph and then tossed her corpse into the fireplace and made smores over it. Needless to say, by August the entire world was at war.

The war may have created a market for soldiers abroad, but back at home there was scarcely a customer since all the men were gone, so what's a tobacco company supposed to do? To create a new local market for their products, Big Tobacco invented Women's Lib and started marketing Marlboro's to the gals as "Mild as May." Lucky Strike caught on fast and began to claim their cigarettes were designed for women as well and as a result they seized 38% of the market. Women's Lib was so successful that between 1925 and 1935 smoking rates among female teenagers tripled. Indeed, they came a long way, baby. In 1939, the Pall Mall was invented, making American Tobacco the largest company in the United States, but thanks to Hitler, all cigarette manufacturers would begin to thrive like never before, when Big Tobacco successfully lobbied for a bill that would insure millions of cigarettes were included in soldier's rations during World War II and those who managed to make it home alive would be loyal customers for life. Business was good for Big Tobacco and that's how it should have been.

In the 1950s, WWII veterans started dropping dead from cancer, so of course the bleeding heart yuppies didn't blame it on the chemical weapons launched by the Nazis—they blamed it on the cigarettes. In 1953, some idiot decided to insulate his pet mice for the winter with tar and low and behold, the little vermin developed tumors, feeding the liberal frenzy against this God granted habit. So Big Tobacco was forced to promote new products that were marketed as "safer" such as the pansy-named Kent that muted the rich taste and aroma with a filter. That wasn't good enough for the democracy-wrecking hoodlums who in 1956 forced Big Tobacco to stop filtering their cigarettes with asbestos. The defenders of our right to smoke had to devise a new scheme to compensate for the fags' war on fags so the menthol cigarette was invented. Menthol cleared the breathing passage ways, allowing people to absorb twice the tar to make up for what they were losing through the filters.

As if an entire decade of attacks by the unbathed welfare-depending pot-smokers wasn't enough, things went really sour in the 1960s when the liberals formed militant gangs called the Flower Children who terrorized our great nation by funking up public places with their body odor. One of these commie pinkos worked for the surgeon general's office and fabricated a report that scared the government into actually regulating the freedom of speech of cigarette advertisements. Health warnings were even planted on packs of cigarettes and the hippies tried to seize the market by making their own utopian version of a cigarette called Bravo that was made out of dried lettuce but of course that failed miserably. By 1971, all television ads for cigarettes were forced off the air.

The war on cigarettes became too much for Big Tobacco to bear, so the companies had to diversify. Phillip Morris bought into the Miller Brewing Company and RJ Reynolds was forced to change its name from Tobacco Company to Industries and it started manufacturing aluminum foil hats for the liberals to wear. As you probably suspect, though, the rest of the 70s was a blur of disco and cocaine so while everyone was distracted, Big Tobacco managed to remain the second most heavily advertised product on the American market.

You could call the 1980s the decade of the opportunists, because that's when all the frivolous lawsuits against Big Tobacco began. Smoking somehow became politically incorrect, with more and more public places banning it. In 1982 some hedonist suggested that second hand smoke may cause lung cancer and suddenly smoking was prohibited even in the workplace. And nobody blamed microwave ovens for the fact that lung cancer became the #1 killer of women — no, of course not, because obviously cigarettes are the only life threatening habit mankind indulges in. As if to add insult to injury, by the turn of the decade smoking was banned on all domestic flights. If you can't even smoke a cigarette in an airplane, where can you smoke?

Phillip Morris was so damaged by this renewed surge of anti-smoking propaganda that it was forced to buy into Kraft and General Foods. Reynolds just went ahead and bought Nabisco outright and invented the Oreo Cookie to appease the NAACP. So the next time you eat your ninety-nine cent box of macaroni and cheese you should be thanking Big Tobacco for it.

You might think all of this negative hoopla from the Ben & Jerry's jihadists would have destroyed Big Tobacco, but never underestimate the power of

American ingenuity. Big Tobacco answered the call to action by outsourcing. It started marketing heavily in third world countries where there is less meddling by (and more opportunity to influence) government officials. As a result, to this day, Marlboro, worth over $30 billion, is tied only with Coca Cola as the world's No. 1 most valuable product brand, and America continues to be a leading producer, growing tobacco in 16 states, with Kentucky and North Carolina accounting for 71% of it.

Now enter the 21st century. The raving, bongo-playing bedwetters have devised a new plot to fling their slingshots at Goliath. They have crudely taken the nicotine out of the cigarettes and are putting it directly into electronic devices and they are vaporizing it. They are infringing upon the hard earned market of a reputable industry that is responsible for financing the revolution, keeping our heroes alert during two world wars, and promoting women's liberation and racial integration. Tobacco was granted to us by God Himself as the answer to the ancient philosophical question: what happens after sex? If God wanted us to vape it, he would have given us circuit boards instead of brains!!

We ask you to show your patriotism by putting down your atomizers and coming back to the loving embrace of Big Tobacco. If you won't do it for yourself, do it for the last remaining American Indians whose ancestors you are insulting with your leafless piss pipes.

Paula M. Clair, Vice Chairman,
Institute for the Preservation
of the Institution of Cigarettes

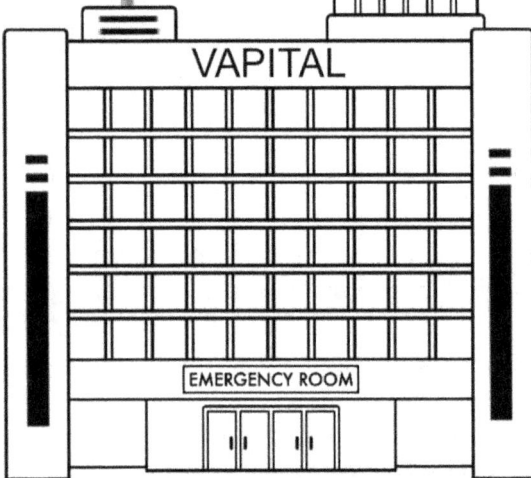

As fate would have it, I was hit by a double whammy. Right after I got banned from Vape Mania all my maxed out credit cards, one by one, were cancelled due to non-payment. I still had a debit card associated with a checking account used for the direct deposit of my disability check, but I only had pennies left after I paid my bills, and without the coupon codes and discount announcements from the forum, I couldn't order anything online. I tried signing up to the website under assumed usernames but somehow they knew and deleted my account before I could get out of the newbie room. I deleted all my cookies and unplugged my modem for a while, thinking my IP address would change so that they couldn't recognize me—but they still knew.

Like a bucket with a hole in it my vaping supplies began to run out. I couldn't even afford to buy new heads for my tanks so I resorted to rebuilding them, wishing I had paid more attention to the forum members who tried in vain to instruct my cynical self on the process. I spent countless hours watching YouTube instructional videos but when I finally sat down to attempt it, I realized I had no kanthal left, so I smashed open my toaster and salvaged the wiring from it. I used cotton from aspirin bottles and Q-tips. Everything tasted like burnt rubber but at least I managed to keep on vaping for the time being.

The juice was another problem. I was running low. I tried dripping all the last drops from my near empty bottles into one bottle to make a goulash of juice and it tasted like minestrone soup thinned with Vicks Vapor Rub but at least it had nicotine in it. Finally, out of desperation, I squirted the last remaining drops under my tongue, rubbed it on my gums, thumbed it onto my eyeballs, and injecting it into my vein with a blunt needle but all that did was make me bleed profusely. Things were looking grim. My shelf was filled with empty plastic dropper bottles and thirsty rubber bulbs.

To my delight I received temporary relief when I found the bottle of Vampire Blood still duct taped to the pad of an electric sander that I intended to use to steep it with, but that didn't have a chance of survival against my eager vapes that sucked until the hit was dry. I found every spent tissue that I used to mop up spilt juice and I smoked them in homemade pipes made out of Reynolds Wrap. The throat hit was out of this world but in due time even that was gone.

My need for a nic-fix starting affecting my work. I started painting children's faces like The Baseball Furies from The Warriors or like Brandon Lee as The Crow. I finally lost all motivation and gave all the children black faces and I assume that offended the weapons dealer working next to me because a complaint was filed and I was fired.

I stood on the expressway ramp with a sign drawn on a piece of cardboard that read "Vapeless. Spare some change for some juice?" and with every sawbuck I scrounged up I bought a cigalike and broke it open to squeeze out the juice into one of my tanks.

With every one of my vaping supplies spent, I broke into Granmama's house and found her sitting at her desktop computer vaping off a Prometheus

RDA attached to a Variable Voltage Janeiro Oakvil. She didn't notice me as I crept up on her and looked over her shoulder. She was logged into Vape Mania under an account named GMILF using a photo of Angela Lansbury as her avatar and she was having a private chat with another member who called himself CarKing.

"What in the blazes are you doing?" I screamed.

She was so startled that her thumb squeezed the plastic bottle in her Janeiro and juice came spraying out of the 510 connector like a little Buckingham Fountain. Halo popped up off her lap and let out an ear splitting yap at me.

"Jesus Mel, what're you trying to do, give me a heart attack?"

"What! Are! You? Doing?" I shouted.

"I'm just chatting with your uncle," she blurted angrily as she snatched some tissues from a box to wipe the juice off her computer screen. Halo jumped to the floor.

"Oh for cart's sake, that's YOU carrying on with Uncle Nick?? You have Virginia all worked up. She thinks he's seeing another woman."

"So what now, I can't even chat with my own son on the webbers?"

I pulled up a chair and sat on it, staring her in the face, and I took her hand into mine. "Granmama. Please tell me that you're not working for that forum."

"A woman my age has to do something with her time."

"This is madness! How did this happen?"

"They have a link right there for job opportunities. Haven't you ever bothered to click on

113

it?"

"You mean to tell me that you're getting paid to be one of the crazy Vape Mania mods?"

"They don't pay me," she said as if it was something noble. "They just give me all the free vaping supplies I need."

I shook my head like a wet dog trying to free myself of the insanity. Then I took a deep breath, counted to ten and snatched the Janeiro out of her hand as Halo started yapping and I stole a massive lung hit off of it. I held the vapor in until there was barely any steam left to exhale. Then I pleaded in desperation, my lips trembling, trying to hold back the tears. "Granmama. Listen to me very carefully. You have to let me back into the site."

"Deary, rules are rules," she said, shaking her head

"But Granmama!" I spat.

"I could lose my job," she insisted. "You were never one for following rules, were you?" She retrieved her Janeiro from my grasp hissing "Give me that" and she took a toot off of it.

"What are you vaping anyway?" I asked, licking my lips.

"Peach Kobbler from Baker Hill," she said with a shrug.

"Gimme some of that!" I insisted.

"Get your own," she growled. I struggled to get the Janeiro out of her hands, sending Halo into a frantic fit, but Granmama pinched the tender flesh between my thumb and finger with her old claws. "You're not putting your lips on my drip tip," she asserted. "Besides, we all know how you hate vaping mite shit."

"You've got to let me back into Vape Mania," I demanded.

"Why should I?" she rebutted with hostility.

"If you don't, I'll let everyone know that you use Scrabble Finder when you play Words with Friends," I threatened.

"You wouldn't!"

"Try me!" I tempted victoriously.

She considered this for a moment and then laughed, "Right, like Alice knows how to spell sequoia. They all do it."

My jaw dropped. "How could you do this to me?"

"They think you're a troll working for the antz," she explained.

"Antz? What are antz?" I cried.

"Anti-Nicotine Zealots," she answered.

"I'm not an ant!" I insisted. "Listen, you old bag, you have to let me back into the site this instant."

"Deary, I couldn't get you back in even if I wanted to. A lifetime ban is irreversible."

I was petrified. I reached down to pet Halo in search of some comfort and she snarled at me. I rose up from my chair in horror. I barely remember walking away from Granmama like a zombie; all I remember is slamming her door behind me.

As I was walking through Oriole Park with the low flying jets screaming above my head, I felt it coming on with a confusing mixture of contradictory emotions: *the vape ABCs*. I felt abandoned as I shielded my eyes from the sun with my trembling, pale hands. I couldn't tell what was north or south as I accepted my fate, feeling affection for the cooing pigeons pecking breadcrumbs. But then I became agitated and aggressively jumped into the middle of them, amazed by their instant flight. As I walked away nauseous, they merely came down behind me and gathered again and this angered and annoyed me although as I passed through the children's play lot, I felt aroused and then ashamed. I was astonished that my headache could be worse than it already was, bewildered by the sweat that came out of my pours as if my skin was nothing but marine grade micron mesh. I jumped at every chirping bird as I see-sawed between feeling bitter and bubbly. Someone was asking me what I was doing there but all I could say was "Vape, vape?" not able to focus on a single thought, my words sounding as if they were coming from a distance.

The loss of Vape Mania dawned upon me and I felt crushed. No, it's not lost, I told myself, I can rent a computer at the Fed Ex Kinkos and use the forum from there—nobody would recognize me. When I realized that I didn't have any money to do that I felt embarrassed and enraged, talking to myself and shouting nonsense. I was struck by a fit of euphoria and I danced like Fred Astaire and cinematically ran up the sliding board and then slid down on my side striking a pose. People didn't seem impressed; in fact they seemed terrified. Some of them were grabbing their children and frantically poking their cell phones with their fingers and I felt a pain in my hip and realized I had injured myself. I felt foolish and limped away as the gloom overcame me.

I was the one who turned Granmama onto the juice and I felt guilty. I hated Vape Mania although at the same time I felt heartbroken that it had rejected me. I felt homesick, wanting to be with my vaping family. I was hopeful that I could find a way back in, but then I remembered how the moderators treated me, and I felt humiliated and I went hysterical, running from the park and digging with my fingers at the flowers in a bed next to a brick building, sending them flying in pieces between my legs. I had a moment of inner peace when I saw the flowers belonged to the copshop, but then my mind swayed and I felt a bout of jealousy toward those who were still allowed into the forum, who were getting their juice for pennies and who were winning free stuff through all the contests. Maybe if I made another attempt at signing up and expressed nothing but kindness I would be liberated from this exile. But I knew I was only fooling myself and I mourned the loss and needed a hug and felt offended when people shoved me and cursed at me when I tried to give them one. They were all going to call the cops, I realized, and I suddenly became panicky and paranoid, regretful for what I had done, although still selfish enough to wonder how I could get some e-juice out of it.

Then I heard a whistling like a radiator blowing steam coming from the sky. I looked up and a big white cloud formed and then dissipated within seconds. Again I heard the whistling scream, this time accompanied by a gurgling as if I was surrounded by lava. I was tormented by the noise and as I looked to the horizon in terror, I saw over the rooftops a fifty foot tall Genny on a telescopic mod, its button blinking like a traffic barricade. It had a hand blown art glass drip tip for a head and it was wielding two pen style carto arms that blew exhaust like chimneys up into the air. It thundered out into the street before me on cigalike legs, the pink juice inside of it swaying back and forth like baby oil. I shook off my uneasiness and shouted up at the beast, "Vape Mania, I'll get my revenge!" but the creature roared and smashed a house to pieces as if it was made of packing peanuts and cotton balls. I ran for dear life through the traffic with horns honking and people screaming until I was worn-out and could only collapse on the sidewalk, yearning to take a puff off the monster.

I must have passed out for a while because when I came to, I was covered in dimes and pennies and some pigeons were walking around on me and as my vision cleared I looked up at the brick and mortar storefront before me. There was a neon sign glowing purple in the window.

It read ZestyD's Vape Shop.

All the vape shops in all the towns in all the world, I had to wake up in front of ZestyD's. I scooped up the change from the sidewalk and collected it in my fedora and entered the vape shop as if in a dream, the door activating a tiny collection of wind chimes. I looked around in amazement. The walls were lined with shelves upon shelves of different bottles of e-juices. Under the display counter was every tank and mod known to mankind. Al Green's Let's Stay Together was softly piped down from the ceiling. In the back of the cramped space was a lounge area that looked like the inside of the magic bottle from I Dream of Jeannie. A short woman in a sweater with straight black hair and thick glasses with plump legs sticking out of a red pleated skirt stood behind the counter smiling at me with a mouthful of braces.

"Where's ZestyD?" I hissed through my clenched teeth.

"That's me," she said, smiling like The Cheshire Cat.

"You. You're ZestyD?" I asked. I looked behind her to see the banner that read Exclusive Midwest Supplier of Baker Hill products. "How's business?" I asked condescendingly.

Her smile faded a bit. "Well you know," she said meekly, "it could always be better." The infinite animosity that had been harboring inside of me crashed down into my intestines and I was overwhelmed with a mixture of disillusionment and sadness.

"What would you recommend?" I asked cautiously.

"What are you into?" she asked. "Fruits, tobaccos, mints, desserts?"

"Your most complex flavor."

She smiled and her face scrunched up, accepting my challenge. She turned around and pointed her finger at the shelves of juices, waving it around and walking forward as if pinning a tail on a donkey and she climbed up on a step stool and retrieved a cobalt blue bottle. "This one's good," she said and showed it to me.

"Albino Eyes," I said with a nod, "of course."

"Do you want to try it? I have a tank prefilled." She offered me a basket of sterilized drip tips and I chose a long titanium one and popped it into the tank that was attached to a simple ego-style battery. I took a skeptical vape and was amazed to feel a near orgasm. The flavor was rich, like a perfectly baked potato with slightly burnt skin cut open and filled with sour cream and sharp cheddar cheese with just a hint of bacon bits. "That's amazing," I said.

"You have to steep that one. When it's fresh it tastes like doo doo. But after about two months —"

"Two months?" I guffawed. "Really?"

"Good things are worth the wait," she assured me. "It takes a while for all the flavors to bond with each other. If you'd like something a bit simpler —"

"No, no," I said. "Do you think I could —" and I gestured with my jaw toward the lounge area.

"Please do," she said happily.

I sat on a love seat in the little circle of tasseled pillows and lava lamps, surprised that there was nobody else there. I had always imagined vape lounges would be filled with intellectuals uppitily vaping as they discussed James Joyce's Ulysses. ZestyD sat across from me at the coffee table curiously observing me as I vaped the Albino Eyes.

"You seem so nice," I said.

She blushed and adjusted her pop bottle glasses. "Thank you."

"Don't you think the internet has a tendency to bring out the nastiness in people?" I asked, savoring a thick flow of vapor that hovered at the back of my throat and serpentined out of my nostrils.

"I suppose," she said. "It's probably due to the anonymity. People are more inclined not to self-censor when there aren't any consequences."

"I was standing in a line at the post office the other day, trying to find out what happened to my lost vape mail, and I was the only one there whose head wasn't bowed down, looking at a flip phone."

"Makes you wonder what's so urgent that they sacrifice the here and now for it."

"A picture of a cute kitten on Facebook," I answered.

She let out a little chipmunk's giggle. "Something shiny perhaps?"

I laughed and coughed out a blast of stacked baked potato. "Oh my, was that green onion I just tasted? It's so subtle."

"Chives. I find Albino Eyes a little buttery myself," she said.

I took a mouth hit and wiggled my tongue around in it. "Salted butter," I confirmed.

"If you like that, you should try the Lime in the Coconut."

"Doesn't have much of a throat hit though," I

remarked.

"It's only twelve milligrams of nicotine. New city ordinance put a cap on it."

"How much is a bottle of this?" I asked.

"Comes to about fourteen dollars with tax," she said.

"Must be a huge bottle," I said.

"Sorry, that's for the twelve milliliter. They're taxing it like tobacco now, you know — "

"New city ordinance," I said, finishing her sentence. I breathed in, content with the nicotine I had absorbed. I gently placed the tank on the table and sat back. "I feel really bad wasting your time," I said, "but this is all I have," and I let her look into my fedora.

"Not at all," she said with constrained gusto. "Now that you know I'm here, come and visit me again."

"I will," I said, spilling the change into my palm and sliding it into the pocket of my overcoat. "Well, I guess I should be moving along."

As I was making my way toward the door, ZestyD called out to me. "Listen, take this!" She approached and handed me a flier.

"What's this?"

"It's an invitation to a vape meet," she said, "happening this afternoon."

"No thanks. I've been to one of these CAVE meetings," I said. "It's not all that."

"No, no, this is just a meeting for people who are curious about vaping. These things are usually filled with vendors giving out free samples. It's like Trick or Treating," she giddily assured me.

"Really?" I said. "Thank you." I looked her in the

eyes almost hoping to find something evil and sinister there, but found nothing but sincerity.

As I left the vape shop with the wind chimes jangling, ZestyD called out, "Have a good vape!"

The IPIC Amnesty Program

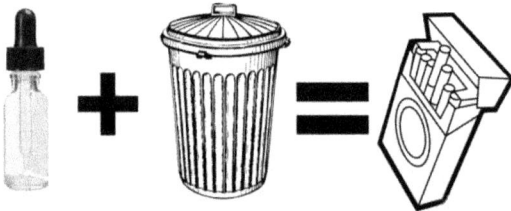

Receive a pack of smokes for every 15ml of e-juice,
Some restrictions may apply; details at your local Snake Eyes store.

PUFF 14

The flier for the vape meet led me to the Exploration Center, a three story brick structure with ornamental gargoyles on the firewalls, a giant honeybee etched into a slab of limestone over the front double doors and two identical statues of an owl wearing a monocle at either side of the entryway. I entered and asked the deskman if he knew what room the vape meet was in, but the guy had a hard time understanding me even with his bicycle seat hearing aid, so I moseyed on up the marble stairs and started searching door by door.

Some of the meeting rooms had signs on the door identifying them: Yoga, Tupperware, Amvets, Alcoholics Anonymous, Shoplifters of the World Union, but I couldn't find one that said Vape Meet, so I went up a narrower flight of stairs to the third floor. The doors up there had no signs on them. I found a scratch mark in the fogged glass of one of the doors and put my eye up closed and peeked through. A man in a goatee wearing a long white gown was crouched in front of a woman sitting on a wooden stool. He was twirling around what looked to be a glittering crystal at the end of a string that he pinched in his fingers. "When I count to ten, you will be in a deep, deep sleep," he said.

I went to the next door and couldn't see in, so I held my ear to it and I heard someone describing something. "This one is nine inches long when the battery is installed. It's self-dripping when you squeeze this." I held up my thumb in approval and quietly opened the door only to find a woman who looked like John McCain in drag holding up a thick black vibrating dildo, giving it a squeeze to demonstrate how it squirts. My mouth instinctually popped open and my tongue rolled out and I stepped back and ever so gently shut the door undetected and then rubbed my eyes with my fists.

I tip-toed to the next and put my ear to the door and I overheard a conversation between several individuals. "Put the tip between your lips." "There, now very gently draw it into your throat." "Squirt it right in there." I nodded my head and opened the door and saw a massive pile of naked bodies wriggling like a blob of live bait on a thick blue wrestling mat. I stood there in the sliver of the door's opening, gawking, wondering if it could be some type of sex therapy class. The aroma of sweat wafted thickly at me so I eased the door shut and began walking toward the next one, but an idea came to me. The mound of flesh that I had just witnessed seemed so deeply absorbed in the activity at hand that I doubt any of the participants were paying attention to anything outside of their intercourse and certainly wouldn't notice if a new appendage slipped into the mix. I skillfully reopened the door without making so much as peep and crept up on what looked like contracting and expanding suckers on the tentacles of a massive octopus. I unzipped my fly and pulled myself out and was about to mount a random pair of flopping buttocks when half of a thick mustached face emerged from the squirming flesh like a Cyclops and smiled at me. "No clothes allowed, but you can keep your hat on." It was then I saw there wasn't a single female in the pile. I staggered back, the words "Sorry I must have the wrong room" blurting from me like a kick to the knee. I tripped on my own two feet back into the hallway and in my haste I zipped up over my foreskin and spent the next few minutes freeing myself.

I was about to give up when I looked down the hall to the last door and saw a rather obvious sign that read VAPE MEET.

I entered this last room quietly but for some reason everyone was alert and turned to look at me. They were standing around eating cheese and crackers. "Come on in," a tall woman in a business suit called to me, gesturing for me to close the door behind me. "We're just getting started." She stepped up to a podium and this seemed to be a signal for everyone to take their seat, so I did the same. No two people in the room looked alike. There was an old woman with pointy eyeglasses with rhinestones glued to the frames, a young man with his first facial hair proudly protruding in solitude between the dimple and pimple on his chin, a man in greasy coveralls with the name José stitched to it, an overweight woman with no neck in a wheelchair and, and, there was Francesco Constantine, sitting there with the rest of them. I *pssted* toward him a few times before he finally acknowledge me. He shook his head discreetly and shushed me and then turned back to look at the woman at the podium.

"My name is Joy," she said, "and I'm a vapoholic." Everyone started laughing, whistling, hooting and clapping. Seems they thought her nicotine addiction was a joke for some reason. "I smoked two packs a day for twenty-five years. I've now been vaping for four months and haven't had a single analog." Everyone cheered and called out words of congratulations. "I don't cough any more, my taste buds are back, my clothes don't stink like a an ashtray, I can jog up a flight of stairs without wheezing, my husband doesn't mind kissing me anymore, my every breath isn't giving people around me cancer and I've saved about a thousand dollars."

She waited until the applause subsided before she continued. "Today we have with us representatives from juice chefs Rip Vape Winkle, The Three Vapeteers and Peter Pan Vapery. We'll have a demonstration of the new Spitfire 510 Rebuildable Self Contained Nukomizer from Charlotte's Vape and our keynote speaker this afternoon will be Franz Pöschl of Warlock Labs who will be giving a demonstration on D I Y."

"What's D I Y?" I whispered to the black man sitting next to me.

He turned to me momentarily and said "Do it yourself," and then his head popped back like a spring toward the woman at the podium.

"So before we get started," she announced, "let's have a vape. Our guest vendors will be passing out free 3ml samples from a variety of their selections and if you didn't bring your own PV there are some atomizers on the table over there. Please return the drip tips to the vodka bowl before you leave."

Everyone started getting up and mingling with the vendors. "So that's it?" I asked. "Now we get free stuff?"

"Isn't it great?" the guy next to me laughed as he got up to get some samples.

"It sure is," I said in amazement. "I can't believe I haven't heard of this before."

I made it a habit of keeping my own atty on me at all times, so I began mingling and accepting freebies that I dripped and tooted, slowly working my way nonchalantly toward Francesco Constantine, who was asking an awful lot of questions and collecting as many samples as he could, dropping them all into a big ziplock bag. I managed to get next to him and we feigned some idle chatter until we could ease ourselves away from the rest of the crowd.

"So you've taken up vaping?" I whispered, failing to maintain my hostility.

"Shhh," he said out of the side of his mouth like a skilled ventriloquist. "I'm undercover. You're going to give me away."

"Listen," I urged with desperation in my voice while maintaining a relaxed smile. "I've been totally cut off. I can't find a cheap vape anywhere."

"Think of it as a blessing," Francesco Constantine said. "Do you know where that tank you gave me is made?"

"I know, it's made in China, so is everything at Walmart."

"Sure, the thing was assembled in China, but it was designed in Japan by a firm allegedly associated with the yakuza and the main American distributor is in New Jersey, owned by some guy named Rocco Mastrantonio. Doesn't that sound dubious?"

"What the hell do I care where it's made? I need a fix. It's driving me batty." I dripped three more drops of Joosy Fruit into my atomizer and put on a cheap acrylic drip tip and took a vape. "Do you know I got banned from Vape Mania," I said, pausing to blow out a cloud, "for bringing up what you told me about the mite shit?"

"Funny you should mention Vape Mania," he said softly, smiling and nodding at those who meandered by. "The mystery deepens. That website isn't even located in the United States. Their main server is located in Myanmar."

"Are you even listening to me? What do I care where their server is? I was getting my vaping supplies for next to nothing through them."

"Well why did you bring up the mite feces anyway? I told you that was the least of your concerns. It's all that other stuff that's in there that you should be worried about."

"You don't think I should be worried about mite shit?" I squealed. People looked at me as the two of us regained our composure. "Say, listen," I said, pulling aside one of the vendors. "This juice tastes great but I'm not getting much of a kick out of it. What gives?"

"I imagine you wouldn't," he said. "It's zero nic."

"What do you mean, zero nic?"

"It's zero nic. New city ordinance forbids vape meets from distributing free samples of nicotine products."

"So you're saying there's no nicotine in this?" He nodded. "You mean to tell me it's legal to have a homorgy down the hall there but we can't sample nicotine products?"

"Calm down," Francesco Constantine urged.

"Why would anyone want to vape zero nic?"

"For the flavor," he half answered, half asked. "It's what you're working toward anyway," he said, giving me a pat on the shoulder, "isn't it? To completely kick the habit?"

"Oh for the love of glassomizers!" I cried out. The vendor excused himself and made his way toward a group of people oohing and awing over his product.

"Mr. Provario," Francesco Constantine whispered. "I told you the mite feces was just the product of unsanitary lab work."

"Right, you said Baker Hill was unsanitary."

"No, okay, I see where you're coming from. There seems to have been some misunderstanding," Francesco Constantine said. "When I first started doing this research, I didn't have access to the university lab. I had to set up shop in my own kitchen—"

"OHWwoo!!! Hold on," I said, feeling the blood pumping through my temples. "You're trying to tell me the mite shit didn't come from Baker Hill's dirty lab," I said and Francesco Constantine nodded, smiling at the group who was now beginning to take their seats for the demonstration. "You're telling me the mite shit came from *your* lab?"

"Bingo," he said. "I actually had to retest that sample at the university, you know, due to the contamination."

"Francesco," I said, setting my bottle of zero nic juice down and pocketing my atomizer. "I need to have a word with you outside."

"But the D I Y demonstration," he said.

"Don't worry. This won't take but a minute." I wrapped my arm around the back of his neck like he was my best friend and guided him out of the room into the hallway. Then I closed the door to the meeting room, stepped back, took a breath and karate chopped Francesco Constantine squarely on the Adam's apple. He stumbled back, gagging.

"How's that for a throat hit!?" I hollered at him and punched him in the nose, blood instantaneously gushing from his face. "You motherfloodin' piece of silica," I screamed and I charged at him, kneeing him in the stomach. He keeled over. I stepped back and brought my foot up, striking him on the jaw. He went stumbling backwards, rolling against the wall, leaving a trail of blood. I reached into my pocket and took out my Aga T3 RBA, bouncing its heft in my palm, and I threw it at him. It ricocheted off his forehead, leaving a gaping red indentation that dribbled blood down into his eye. He fell back through the doorway and floundered down the stairwell like a pile clothes. I came marching down with my hands like vices in front of me, my eyes glaring like a pair of headlights. I leapt down onto him like a professional wrestler, my knees landing on his chest, and I wrapped my hands around his throat.

"Stop, stop," he pleaded through bubbles of blood. "You're killing me."

"Just answer one question for me, you cartosucking floodin' attyhole piece of wick," I said, tightening my grip. "Is vaping healthier than smoking or isn't it?"

"It, it, it all depends on your perspective," he gurgled and coughed.

"Answer the question!!" I growled.

"Yes," he cried. "Of course it is. But that doesn't mean it's *safe*."

I let loose of his throat, tossing him down like a wet rag. I got up and wiped the blood from my hands with a juice stained handkerchief and then flung it onto his face. I adjusted my fedora and when

I turned there he stood, with one foot on the hallway floor and the other on the marble stairway. It was Triton, with his well-trimmed red hair and sissy earring and checkerboard shirt, standing there gawking at me.

"YOU!!!" I roared, causing everyone behind every door to shuffle and gasp.

Triton zipped away down the stairs like a startled deer and in a mad fury I was in hot pursuit.

USA **49**

United We Smoke

Celebrate the Anniversary of
Big Tobacco with this
Sestercentennial
Commemorative Stamp

I came storming out of the Exploration Center just in time to see that flooder Triton slip into one of those pansy ass powder blue Flash Cabs. Across the street I saw some driptip probably on his way to the anal logging meet parking his fully restored tits 1970 Ford Boss 302 Mustang. I pulled out my iTaste MVP2 with a Kanger Mini Protank attached to it and held it as if it was a pistol, barking, "Get on the ground you son of a bridge!" The stupid dolt obeyed and I ran up to him pointing my tank at his face. "Give me the keys!" I snatched them like a clam popping and hopped into his car.

"You're not getting away from me this time, Triton!" I hollered, driving over the curb onto the sidewalk to avoid traffic, smashing into an old man's Mariano's shopping cart filled with metal scraps. I plowed between two parked cars with a rain of sparks and sideswiped a hippie driving a Volkswagen Bug that spun to the side like a poker chip smashing into a light pole.

In my rage I yanked the stick around and worked the clutch as if it was nothing but a square dance. The beast I was driving had some power too. Its engine roared like an earthquake and I was catapulted over a speed bump like a native's striped spear, landing and bouncing on rubber like a speedboat hitting the waves. I saw the taxi take a right under the el tracks onto Lake Street and in no time I was pulling the steering wheel and slamming on the brake, making the turn with an elephant's scream and a cloud of smoke, ripping off the passenger side mirror on something big and sturdy that flashed by like a mirage. The taxi managed to get through the light before it turned red but I didn't hesitate, plowing through the flexible posts of the protected bike lane into the intersection where I nearly struck a woman carrying a baby who came at me as close as the final frame of Sunset Boulevard. While avoiding her I was propelled into an out of control skid into the front of a Snake Eyes convenience store with a massive splash of glass and slushy blue iced beverage.

I put it in reverse like stirring a soup and yanked the car out of the Snake Eyes, screaming back onto Lake Street and getting rear ended by the side of a city bus, and then I blasted off with a burn out that left black marks on the pavement like Kilroy's eyes. I punched it, the el tracks above sending beams of light flipping against the cracked windshield as the rush of wind from my furious vehicle kicked up the paper and dirt in its track. I saw the taxi way up ahead taking a left onto Pulaski, so I floored it with abandon like the Starship Enterprise engaging warp speed and I laughed maniacally as I approached the intersection within seconds but then my right front tire hit a pot hole as big as a meteorite crater and the car popped up and crashed back down like a rock skipping across water. In an immeasurable flash I went dashing through the intersection and up the ramp of a UHoard truck filled with antique furniture, smashing through wood and glass and ripping through the far end of the trailer, the bottom of the Mustang exploding across the top of the cab with a splash of oil and fire and transforming me into a state of zero gravity until I came down like a wood chisel gouging out the earth to a violent dead stop against a fire hydrant with a blast of water and radiator steam.

I rolled out of the totaled vehicle, checking my pockets to make sure my vape gear was okay. As police sirens wailed in the distance, I staggered to the intersection just in time to see Triton exiting the taxi a block and a half down. He was calmly paying the driver and thanking him and then he casually walked off the sidewalk and out of sight. I ran as best as I could, the Mustang blowing clouds into a gush of water that shattered into the el tracks above, raining down all over the street behind me.

The only place he could have gone was through a narrow gangway between two frame houses sided with rotted asphalt. I limped to the backyard where there was a muscular pit bull restrained by a rather flimsy chain trying its best to tear me apart. I slipped between a rundown brick garage and a chain link fence into the back alley, looking this way and that and discovering footprints in the mud. I use to work at the Megaplex, so I know a thing or two about the shape of Salvatore Ferragamos. There was only one person who would be slopping through this ghetto wearing eight hundred dollar shoes. I followed Triton's tracks to a dead end where there was a flat steel door flush with the wall of the seemingly abandoned factory building, with no means to open it except for an oversized key slot.

I waded through the weeds around the building, climbing over chunks of cement and bricks, kicking away a dead rat that went spinning comically through the air. I noticed the fire escape and darted like a seasoned free runner up the wall, grabbing it to pull it down. I went up and knocked out a section of window with my elbow, reached in and unfastened the lock, pulling the window out and squeezing through and rolling onto the floor, finding myself in darkness. I crept in a silent crouch toward a doorway that had dull light coming from it that left a distorted yellowish film over the floor. As I approached there he was, Triton, in a little room with a pencil tucked behind his ear, sitting at a desk between stacks of brown boxes with mailing labels on them. He was punching away on an adding machine that spat out a strip of paper. As I took a step closer he sensed my presence and looked at me, only able to see my silhouette.

"Who's there?" he demanded.

"It's me," I cackled, "your little vape whore."

"Stop. Don't come any closer," he threatened.

I took another step closer. "How huge is this conspiracy anyway?" I scowled.

"I'm serious, don't take another step," he desperately warned, rising up off his chair with frightened eyes.

I took another step closer. "Why me? What part do I play in this demented vaping game of yours?"

"Watch out!" he called out shrilly.

I took another step and fell straight down through a trap in the floor, my feet slamming against rickety open stairs below. My legs buckled with the violent impact and my body broke through the railing and I plunged down head first, landing into a huge vat of maroon colored e-juice with a thick, slimy splash. The liquid filled my mouth and burned my eyes as I struggled to the surface, coughing and spitting as I splashed around desperately in slowed motion in the thick syrupy solution. There was a loud clack and flood lights came on. Triton came walking down the stairs looking at me and shaking his head in disbelief. I tried to swim to the side of the vat but my feet slipped around like a newborn horse.

"Stop it," Triton demanded. "Just stay still."

I flailed about, splashing e-liquid everywhere, gurgling and blowing juice bubbles and calling out to the vape gods to save me. I managed to get to the side of the vat and as I tried to climb out I inadvertently pressed down on a button, activating an engine powering a vacuum pump that forced e-juice to rush from jets, making the e-juice whirl around in a bubbling tide with me trapped in it.

"Your making your juice in a Jacuzzi!" I cried out.

"Do you have a better way to mix and steep at the same time?" Triton shouted back.

"Get me out of this thing," I pleaded as I swept around like a log in the rapids.

"Just stand up!" Triton shouted.

"What??" I cried.

"Just stand up! It's only three feet deep you moron," Triton cursed.

I stopped flailing and managed to stand up in the swirling foam and I walked to the side of the whirlpool and pressed down on the button, settling the juice. Then I lifted my leg over and slipped out, landing on my side where I bounced around like a fish trying to escape. I managed to get to my knees. "Uuuugh," I moaned, "I'm dying."

"You're not dying," Triton said.

"The nicotine," I gasped. "It's absorbing through my skin. It's killing me."

"That's just a flavor base," Triton scoffed.

139

"There's no nicotine in it yet." This calmed me down a bit. I stood up, squeegeeing the juice off my face with the side of my hand. "Why don't you stop self-medicating and seek some professional help," Triton said earnestly.

"Wait a second," I said, tasting the juice that was on my tongue. "I recognize this."

"No you don't," Triton blurted in a hissy fit.

"Yes I do," I said, wiping gobs of juice off my clothes and skin. "This is Vampire Blood!" Triton's mouth opened but he could only stutter and spit out noises. "Funny. Tasting it on my tongue like this, I can make out the flavor profile. It has a bit of black cherry in it, doesn't it."

"Stop it!" Triton said.

"Is that cinnamon redhots? And tell me that isn't bacon. What kind of tobacco flavoring is it? RY4?"

"You're insane!"

"So who are you making this stuff for? Dracula Vision or Dracula Vapor?"

"Vision, Vapor, E-Smoke, Nic-Juice, what's the difference?"

"You mean they're all the same? They're selling the same thing under different names?"

"That's how capitalism works, mate. You have to create generics for those who can't afford the name brand." I felt as soggy as my clothes with disillusionment. "Look what you've done! You've contaminated the entire lot," Triton said angrily. "What are you even doing here?"

"Do you know who I am?"

"Right, you're the bloody psycho who's been stalking me."

"That just goes to show how much you know," I

laughed, "because I haven't been stalking you. I bet the public would like to know about this," I threatened, reaching into my pants pocket and pulling out a glob of Vampire's Blood.

"Who gives a turd," Triton blasted. "As long as they get their juice what do they care where it comes from? Now get out of here."

"Give me some of this," I warned, "at 36 milligrams of nic, or I'll expose your entire sleazy operation."

"I don't have nicotine here you twat. I just make the flavor base. The vendors mix it on demand. You know that."

"You're the one who got me hooked on this," I accused.

"I never told you to stop taking your bloody meds."

"Give me some juice and I'll, I'll, I'll suck your wick," I proposed audaciously.

Triton laughed. "As much as I would love to have my fantasy fulfilled of a juice drenched pillock knobbing me, I - don't - have - any. I only vape zero nic, I swear."

"I can't take it anymore," I said matter-of-factly. "I can't suffer this miserable existence one more second without some juice." I looked toward the big window at the far side of the room.

Triton read my mind and said, "Don't even think about it, mate. That's three stories down."

I calmly placed my fedora on my head, e-juice pouring from it over my face. "I don't care," I said and I ran straight to the window without so much as a pause. I went through with a splatter of glass, hurling down in a euphoric state knowing that my misery would soon be over. But I merely landed with a bounce into an open dumpster filled with bubblewrap scraps.

As I lie there looking up I could see Triton poking his head out of the broken window, looking down at me and shaking his head. "Get some help, mate," he called out.

Black cherry. Redhots. Bacon. RY4. Could it be that simple?

I set out to make everything right. When I received my disability check instead of paying my rent and bills I decided to make an investment in a large quantity of D I Y Vampire Blood that I would then sell online to recoup my losses. First I made a trip to the northwest side and bought a good supply of overpriced juice with my debit card from ZestyD, just to keep my head level as I thought this thing through; and good thing for her I did, because she was suffering from a severe case of the niccups that for some reason were instantly cured when she took a look at me.

I would need some antifreeze—a lot of it. And some skin moisturizer. And some nicotine. And of course the flavoring. I searched online for places to purchase these items and discovered Globalactic Industries, a major supplier of farm implements, where I ordered ten gallons of XFrost Premium industrial coolant for only $120 with free shipping. Next I ordered fifty pounds of skin moisturizer from Apothecary-R-US for only $24 plus $96 shipping. Getting the nicotine proved to be more of a challenge however. As of the first of the year, nicotine based pesticides were completely banned as my luck would have it, but I finally found a website written entirely in Thai that when I Google-translated offered three hundred milliliters of pure nicotine for USA$49.00 plus USA$150 shipping. After I placed my order, the friendly Thai salesman was even kind enough to email me to inform me in broken English that he was throwing in a free gas mask to make up for what promised to be slow delivery since my order needed to be routed through Israel first to avoid customs. By my calculations, for an investment of $440, I ordered enough ingredients to make about 57,000 milliliters of e-juice at 2% nicotine strength that when sold for $10 for a 30 ml bottle would rake in a clean $19,000.

I was on the road to recovery. As I waited for my supplies to arrive by mail I began concocting my flavor base. I went to the dollar store and synchronicity was on my side. There they were, stacked in a big cardboard box with a half price clearance sign on them, bag after bag of Cinnamon Fire Jolly Ranchers. The only issue with them seemed to be that they were all sticky. I made several trips to the checkout with armfuls of candy bags, getting about 120 pounds of them for a measly $20. Carrying them home proved to be quite a chore. I filled up a city trash container with them and knocked it over and tried to roll it but it only wanted to roll around in circles, so I had to stick my fingers through the mesh and drag it, walking backwards the entire way.

My self-confidence must have impressed the vape gods because next I found myself in Stosh's discount produce store right in time to catch them as they were tossing their supply of 39 cent-a-pound cherries in the trash. At first I thought about stopping the Pollack who was hauling them to the alley to make the store an offer for them, but then I thought, why should I do that? Instead I just waited for the market to close and then I dumpster dove, filling my briefcase and all my pockets as well as four shopping bags to the brim with rotted cherries. Sure they had flies on them and had all sort of other garbage mixed in with them, but my intention was to filter the flavor base through cheesecloth anyway, so it would all come out eventually.

I was brainstorming what I could use for the bacon flavor and then some ideas came to me, so back to the dollar store I went and I got twelve bottles of generic hickory liquid smoke for a buck each and I also found some old dusty bottles of Capella's Graham Cracker Flavor Concentrate tucked behind a shelf of assorted spices, knowing they were waiting there in the shadows for who knows how many years and were destined to be mine. The way I figured it, RY4 flavoring is just graham cracker and caramel anyway. So to finish off my list of ingredients, I bought a bottle of pure caramel extract from The Flavor Shack, which was rather pricey but I was overwhelmed with zeal at finding all the ingredients I needed.

Next I needed something to dissolve it together, so I went to the Foremost and got the five biggest jugs of Dimitri vodka I could find. I dumped it all, the vodka, the flavor extracts, the red hot candies (I didn't even bother to unwrap them), the rotted cherries and the liquid smoke into my bathtub. After I did this I kicked myself because it dawned on me that I should have scrubbed the tub out first but everything was going to be siphoned through cheesecloth anyway, so that should get rid of the pubic hairs and soap scum. I took off my shoes and stomped in it, crushing the cherries into juice. And I let it sit there from then on and didn't bathe, stirring my concoction every half hour with a toilet scrubber. It was dissolving and blending together nicely, the plastic wrappers floating to the surface.

My antifreeze arrived in a rather large blue plastic barrel that wouldn't fit through the thin opening of the elevator so I rolled it, step by step, up the stairs. The neighbor who lives below me heard the thumping noise and rapped her broom against the stairwell door, startling me. The barrel slipped out of my grasp and went tumbling down the stairs, the top of it popping off and splattering antifreeze everywhere. In a frantic rush I got my own broom and dustpan and started sweeping up as much of it as I could to pour it back into the barrel. People kept coming down and slipping so I put a sign up that read Stairs Out of Order Use Elevator. I guess that didn't play with that broom happy woman because I heard the blaring sound of fire trucks honking their horns as they approached. Firemen came rushing in and confronted me as I frantically swept up my precious antifreeze. They told me that my neighbor had reported a chemical spill but I assured them it was nontoxic, and I wiped some up with my fingers and sucked it off to demonstrate. The fire marshal was rather agitated, but I promised him it would be cleaned up by nightfall and they left me alone.

I didn't realize so many people in the building had cats until I brought my barrel of antifreeze into my room and observed all the hair floating around in it, but it was all going through cheesecloth anyway so I dumped it into the bathtub and stirred it around.

The next day my skin moisturizer arrived, packaged in a metal barrel with its lid tightly pinned closed. This one fell down the stairs as well, as I slipped around on the remnants of the antifreeze, but the metal barrel did not come open. I managed to get it inside, got it opened with a hammer and screwdriver, and dumped it, as thick as molasses, into the bathtub. I turned on the faucet for some water to thin it and stirred it around with a plunger.

The bathtub stayed that way for three weeks while I waited for the nicotine to arrive. I was unable to bathe so I kept spraying myself with Fabreeze. I was so overwhelmed with anticipation that I could barely eat. All I could do was sit at my desk and vape while I watched videos about how to build atomizers, dreaming about the fancy mods I would buy with all the money.

I watched so many videos that I figured I was an expert at it, so I worked on building the world's largest personal vaping device, using a big bell jar for a tank. I invented my own eight coil atomizer that fit snugly into the jar's opening, consisting of wires ripped from a space heater, stainless steel kitchen scrubbing pads, a rolled up piece of wool sweater and a light switch that I recycled from the wall. I duct taped a large metal funnel to it for a drip tip and mounted the entire thing on a tripod. It was hooked up to a series of extension cords that I could simply plug into an outlet whenever I was ready, but I wouldn't be ready until the Dracula Melvin brand Vampire Blood was completed. I held out for that moment to test my MP-5000 0.225 ohm 120 Volt Octacoil Clearomizer with the 1000 milliliter tank.

I was beginning to suspect that my Thai friend had ripped me off, because every time I caught Ernesto the postman coming down the block he was empty handed. Until one day I was called down to the lobby to sign for a package and I eagerly brought it to my bathroom. I cut it open with the little knife from my toenail clippers and was surprised to find inside a rather small container of nicotine. I wondered how this little bit of nicotine could possibly spike my entire bathtub full of e-juice.

The gas mask that was included looked like something straight out of Dawn of the Dead. As I tried to wear it, it kept fogging up as I struggled to breathe through it, so I tossed it aside, opened my jar of nicotine and dumped it like Elmer's Glue into the bathtub.

Next thing I know my eyes were burning and I was struggling to catch my breath and the room was spinning and I crawled out of the bathroom suffering from agonizing stomach cramps. I managed to wriggle around and positioned a fan that blew the fumes out into the hallway but then the fire alarm for the building went off. I could hear everyone running through the halls coughing and gagging.

Once again I heard the fire trucks blaring and honking. I got outside to find the entire building vacated due to what was believed to be a gas leak. To cover my tracks, I kept insisting to the fire marshal that the odor was coming from the basement, and after an entire afternoon of inspections by the gas company they did find a little slow leak and determined the gas must have been building up over a very long period of time. The toxic smell subsided as the nicotine steeped into my juice, so the emergency crews called it a day after the suspicious fire marshal interrogated me for a while; then he left me alone as well.

I got back upstairs and put my gas mask on and stirred my e-juice, but by then I was exhausted, so I figured I'd let it steep overnight and I fell down on my futon and passed out, dreaming of firing up my Octacoil.

When I awoke all I could do was rush to the bathroom. I looked at myself in the mirror that was held together with packaging tape. I was a mess. I hadn't bathed in a month. My face was withered and I had huge black bags under my bulging eyes, so I swooshed my hands around in the e-juice, pulling out pieces of plastic and cat hair and dead flies and cherry pits and cigarette butts, clearing a relatively clean portion of it. I scooped up a glob in my cupped palms and carried it into my room, where I carefully parted my hands, pouring it into my homemade mega tank.

My body quivered with anticipation and some pee squirted out of me in delight. I plugged the extension cord into the wall, then wrapped my lips over the funnel and flipped the switch and sucked. There was a loud zap and my mouth was filled with yummy tasting Vampire Blood. I had done it. It was perfect. I groaned in pleasure as the nicotine pumped through my veins like a bullet train and when my head stopped spinning, I flipped the switch again, but this time the zap was followed by a sudden mushroom of flames followed by an evil sounding *BOOUFF!!!* I screamed and slapped at my head of burning hair, bumping the bell jar with my elbow and knocking over the tripod. The jar hit the floor and shattered, sending flames shooting up with a whoosh to the ceiling.

I ran out of the room shouting "Fire!" through the hallway and I slipped down the stairs on my back like a toboggan. I came rushing out of the building fanning my smoking scalp with my fedora.

Soon the sirens were blaring and honking again as the fire trucks arrived. The fire marshal climbed out of his cab and looked at me and sneered, "You again. Another false alarm I suppose?" but just then there was an ear splitting explosion and my bathroom window up above shattered with a ball of flame that rose up over the building and dissipated into black smoke. The firemen went into action like busy bees and before I could blink my lashless lids they were up on a ladder blowing water into my room. The water caused massive clouds of steam to form that wafted down around us. I heard people commenting: "Is that cinnamon? No it's cherry. I smell bacon." My twenty gallons of Vampire Blood was vaping away all over the neighborhood. I went running around the block following the wind, attempting to huff as much of it out of the air as I could.

When the excitement was finally over I looked up at the black hole that was once my living space and it dawned upon me. Everything that was important to me was lost. My variable voltage mods. My ohm meters. My rebuildable atomizers. My bottom feeders. Even my drip tips.

Someone tapped on my shoulder. I turned around to be met by a uniformed man. "Are you Melvin Provario?" he asked. All I could do was put on my fedora and nod. "Please come with us."

"I'm going to ask you once again," said the man sitting on the edge of the desk, who wore a wind breaker that said ATF on it. "Do you require medical attention?"

"No," I insisted with a shrug, sitting there with a lamp twisted so that it shone in my face. "It just took off my hair is all," and I pinched the top of my fedora and lifted it, scratching my scorched scalp.

"Do you know why we brought you here?" he asked.

Images flashed in my mind: dragging Melany like a shot deer up a flight of stairs; my lovely Yugo passed out on my futon; Francesco Costantine sprawled out on the landing of the Exploration Center; a guy on his knees in the street fearfully relinquishing his keys; a car plowing through the front of a Snake Eyes store; breaking and entering into Triton's loft; beating an old lady over the head with a broom handle; my bathtub full of Vampire Blood exploding into a fireball.

"No," I answered. "I haven't a clue. Where are we?"

"The Wicker Park United States Carrier Annex," said a man in a shirt and tie, who was sitting on a chair behind the desk.

"You mean we're at the post office?" I asked, completely confused.

"My name is Postal Inspector Doral," he said. "And this is Agent Maverick."

"I bet you got a lot of action with a name like that when you were in school," I snorted but Mr.

Maverick wasn't amused. "And who's that?" I asked.

There was a pockmarked jittery old man with awful yellow teeth sitting on another chair against the wall of the small room, fidgeting with his bony knees that pressed against his slacks like turtle shells clutching a plastic water bottle between them. "I'm from the Institute," the bony man squeaked like a mouse.

"Melvin, may I call you Melvin?" I nodded. "Do you know what these are?" Inspector Doral asked as he began unloading a bag of parcels onto his desk.

I hunched forward to observe them. "Hey," I announced, "that's my lost vape mail. I've been waiting for those!"

"Melvin, Mr. Doral says you've been receiving packages like these every day for months, from all over the country. We know what's in them." Maverick said, "Tobacco products."

"No sir. There's no tobacco in any of those packages," I exclaimed.

The room was silent for a moment as the three of them gawked at me.

"This vape stuff," the inspector said, "is walking a very thin line. Are they tobacco products or aren't they?" he speculated as I shook my head adamantly. "We're at a quagmire here," he said. "Every time one of these packages from one of these vape shops is sent through the mail, it gets flagged as suspicious and is held for inspection and this just befuddles us, because the rules aren't crystal clear on this. When we have to spend time trying to figure out if and when the line is being crossed, this ties everything up. I'll be honest with you, Melvin, this vaping thing has become so massive that the United States Mail Service is running about two days late because of it." I shrugged my shoulders. "On the one hand, these are used for smoking, just like cigarettes—"

"Vaping," I corrected.

The inspector waved his hand to silence me. "On the other hand, they aren't technically cigarettes so they don't fall within the definitions of the PACT Act. On the one hand, nicotine is a toxic substance, but on the other hand, most of these packages contain such a minute amount of nicotine that they can't exactly be classified as toxic. On the one hand, they aren't properly labeled for delivery of liquids, but on the other hand there are millions of them in route every day. How are we supposed to combat it, if everyone is simply going to ignore the rules? We'd be tied up for months, would have to spend millions of dollars contacting the places of origin to request they be repackaged. And batteries! Mr. Provario, you're not supposed to send batteries through the mail. But all you vapers are just doing it like it's nothing, thousands upon thousands of them, every day, all over the place, going this way and that."

"Hold on a second," I said. "What does any of this have to do with the fire?"

"We're not here about the fire," Agent Maverick said. "That's something the fire department will contact you about. You didn't set your place on fire on purpose did you?"

"Of course not," I said.

"It wasn't arson was it?"

"Freak accident, could've happened to anyone."

"Then you have nothing to worry about. We're here about this," and he gestured toward the packages.

"So all these packages have been inspected?" I asked.

"We don't have the manpower to inspect every package that gets flagged," Inspector Doral explained. "They get flagged. They sit there. More come in. We don't know what to do with them and we don't have room for them, so they get cleared for delivery. We're lucky if we can actually inspect one out of ten thousand suspicious packages. They sit there and they get cleared, sit there and get cleared, day in and day out, wasting everyone's valuable time."

"Did my packages get cleared?" I asked. The inspector frowned. My mouth began to water. "So, they're mine?" The three men looked at each other, grimacing. "Do you mind if I have a vape then?"

"You can't smoke in here," chimed in the man from the Institute.

"No, let him," said the inspector with a flip of his hand. "I'm curious about this fad."

I plunged forward and gathered up the packages and sorted them by vendor then started ripping them open. I found my missing SmokBot-R and I disassembled it there on the desk. Next I retrieved my lost package of stainless steel mesh and wires. I reached into my London Fog for the drill bit that I carried around with me and with it I wrapped a perfect eight loop microcoil and connected it to the positive and negative posts. Then I reached into my overcoat again and retrieved a tiny pair of scissors and cut off a piece of wire mesh and worked it between my fingers as if rolling a joint and then I took out the little pair of tweezers that I was carrying and held the mesh in it and I used my miniature blow torch to make the mesh glow orange. After it cooled, I twisted my mesh wick through the microcoil and into the tank.

I ripped open a bulging manila envelope and pulled off the bubble wrap from the bottle of kiwi flavored e-juice and unscrewed the top and put the dropper tip onto the wick and squirted some juice on it and then I set it on fire with my blow torch and let it burn out, oxidizing it. Then I filled the tank. I opened the box with the Nickel Plated Telescopic Thunderstorm in it and took it apart and inserted two batteries that I was in the habit of carrying around and put the mod back together and screwed it onto the tank. Then I found my missing package of hand carved wood drip tips and I took a moment to observe them and I selected the nicest one that looked like a totem pole and popped it on the tank. Finally I put my lips to it, pressed the button and took the most fabulous vape of my life. My vapor plowed up toward the ceiling fan like a blast from a steam cleaner.

"You go through all of that just to have a smoke?" Maverick asked.

"It's a vape, not a smoke," I said as I held in the next hit. "Actually I can't believe I just pulled that off without so much as a short."

"Do you mind if I have a cigarette?" the man from the Institute asked.

"There's no smoking in here," the inspector said.

"That's smoking!" the Institute man blurted out like a fog horn, pointing at my PV.

I began scooping up all my new vape toys and I stuffed them into my many overcoat pockets. "You brought me down here just to hand deliver all this stuff to me?" I asked giddily. "Thanks."

"We're not concerned about those packages," Maverick said. "We're concerned about one package in particular."

"Is that right? Which one would that be, pal?" I asked, looking at the packages I hadn't opened yet.

"This one," the inspector said, sliding a slip of paper across the desk toward me. I looked down and saw my own signature on a delivery notice.

"That's your signature right?"

"It appears to be," I said cautiously.

"Unfortunately for you, that was the one in ten thousand."

"The nicotine from Thailand," I deflated. I took another vape from my RBA, fearing that it was about to be taken away from me.

"You actually ordered from a Thailander operating out of Sudan, Mr. Provario," Inspector Doral corrected, "who sold you pure nicotine manufactured in North Korea, extracted from Cuban grown tobacco, which was shipped from Somalia to Israel making stops first in Iran, Syria and then Lebanon. Congratulations, Melvin, you managed to violate seven international trade laws with one single purchase."

"Is that bad?" I asked.

"Each violation has a penalty of ten to twenty years in prison and up to a million dollars in fines so, yes, I'd say it's bad," Agent Maverick said.

"Do they let you vape in prison?" I asked. "I'm just saying, because I know they let you smoke in prison, but, I wonder if they let you vape in prison."

"Melvin," the man from the Institute suddenly

spoke up as if he was controlling the room. "Nobody wants to put you in prison. I'm sure that can be avoided as long as you're willing to give us your full cooperation. Do we all agree on that?"

Maverick and the inspector both smiled at me and nodded their heads.

I took a thirsty pull off the SmokBot-R and got a nasty dry hit that corrupted my mouth with the taste of stainless steel. "Ack. Water, water." I lunged forward and snatched the bottle from between the Institute man's knees and I chugged it and then spit it out at the floor. "Ack. Vodka, vodka."

"Mr. Provario, this can't go on! We can't keep having these packages clogging up the system. We need some firm guidelines, but since we can't go around opening up everyone's mail, we can't show enough evidence to get this thing done. We have to prove what's been going on in this" and he held up his fingers and scratched quotation marks in the air "vaping community of yours."

"What do you need from me?" I asked, fanning my open mouth with my hand.

The Institute man cleared his throat. "Next month there's a Joint Commission hearing on this very subject."

"By my records you've received more, what do you call it?"

"Vape mail," I said sadly.

"You've received more vape mail in the last few months than, well, than anyone else, quite honestly," Inspector Doral explained. "What we need for you to do is to stand before the committee and testify to what products you've been receiving, what's in them, what they're used for."

"And it would help," the man from the Institute said slyly, "if you could add some of your own personal concerns, about how unsafe they are. You know, how there needs to be strict regulations."

"Well that juice is awfully flammable," I offered.

"Stuff like that," he said affectionately.

"You do that for us, and I can guarantee you full immunity regarding your little Sudanese purchase," Agent Maverick promised.

"If I do this thing, do I get to keep all my stuff?" I asked, pointing at the packages.

"Sure, you're free to take your parcels," Inspector Doral sighed.

I shook Agent Maverick's hand and said "Maverick, I think this is the beginning of a beautiful friendship," and then I reached over the desk and shook Inspector Doral's hand and said "May your vapes always be warm ones," and then I looked at the guy from the Institute who was sitting there with his grizzled, liver spotted hand extended for me and, well, eh . . .

PUFF 18

I'm running out of paper. I've been hiding out in my UHoard storage unit, tapping into the electricity of the hallway lights, documenting this story using these, the only paper products I have at my disposal.

When I slip out I wear a fake mustache that I made out of ecowool stuck to my upper lip with melted rubber grommets. I go to the public library to use their free internet service, where I discovered to my relief that my DarthVaper Vape Mania account has been reactivated. I assume Granmama did some finagling.

One day I ran into Damian at the library and he recognized me despite my disguise and he was rather hot headed although he wouldn't tell me why. I don't know if I'm just being paranoid, but I thought I saw him following me on two separate occasions, when I snuck out to use the bathroom at the Snake Eyes down the street and when I went to the river to fish for my supper.

The good news is I'm back. I've promised to be a good forum contributor, not to complain or whine too much, not to start arguments or make accusations without learning the facts first. I'll put up with the nonsense of the moderators and obey the rules and as a result I'll be rewarded with cheap vape gear and the know-how to use it. I've already won one of their contests and instructed them to send my free thirty milliliter bottle of flan flavored e-juice to the address of a house that I know to be abandoned, where I plan to pick it up when I get the chance.

But, at last, the world keeps spinning, and now

even my rent for this storage unit is overdue and I'm on my last package of JEB 1.5s. No, I didn't make it to 100 Puffs. I only made it to 18. I'll consider this my cigalike tale that didn't deliver what it promised but served as a stepping stone to something greater.

Maybe someday I will find myself writing the next chapter in my life but for now I'm just Melvin Provario, vaping junkie, no longer a newbie, about to pull up the garage door before they forcefully evict me.

Oh, and about the Institute. I stick my neck out for nobody. They are a

Peroration

Dear America,

Cigarette smoking has unfairly gotten a bad reputation over the years. There are so many claims against it one would think it's the only thing on the planet causing disease. They call it the leading preventable cause of early ill health and claim it is responsible for 500,000 deaths every year in the United States, but that scary number if looked at closely speaks for itself, because there are currently 314,000,000 people living in America, which means smoking only kills a measly 0.16% of the population annually.

The claim has also been made that no biological system in a smoker's body is spared tobacco's harmful effects. But what they don't talk about is the positive effects of smoking. Although it may be true that a large percentage of smokers will suffer from cancer of the lungs, mouth, pharynx, larynx, esophagus, pancreas, cervix, kidneys, bladder, colon and bone marrow, and suffer from emphysema and chronic bronchitis and cardiovascular diseases such as angina and aneurysms and stroke, early aging and psoriasis, have wounds that are slower to heal, suffer from osteoporosis and infertility, have miscarriages, premature or stillbirths, or have babies with cleft palates or who die of sudden infant death syndrome or who grow up mentally retarded or with behavioral problems, it's still unclear what percentage of actual smokers will die from tobaccosis. There is one statistic that *is* clear however: 100% of smokers enjoy the rich flavor, soothing effects and social perks of smoking a cool stick of tobacco wrapped in paper.

What makes cigarettes so enjoyable to smoke of course is the potent alkaloid called nicotine that is formed in the roots and accumulates in the leaves and that constitutes up to 3% of the dry weight of the tobacco plant. A cigarette yields about 1mg of absorbed nicotine that when smoked acts as a stimulant in mammals. This stimulant effect is the dependence-forming property of tobacco and nicotine addiction is one of the hardest addictions to break, with characteristics similar to heroin and cocaine. There is clearly a demand for this nicotine fix and this is why Big Tobacco has been kind enough to increase the nicotine content of their products over the years to accommodate; in fact, between 1998 and 2005 it was increased nearly 2% every year. There is no doubt about the cause of (and thus who has a right to control) nicotine addiction.

Nicotine is as good as two drugs in one. Its profile can easily be changed from a stimulant to a sedative and back again. For example, if you take short quick puffs, this produces a low level of blood nicotine and stimulates nerve transmissions and enhances the actions of dopamine in the brain, resulting in a speedy rush. However, if you take deep puffs, this produces a high level of blood nicotine and enhances the effects of serotonin and opiate activity, which depresses the passage of nerve impulses, producing a calming, pain-killing effect. So although it is argued that the only therapeutic use of nicotine is in treating nicotine dependency, everyone who uses nicotine to self-medicate knows that it treats a wide variety of life's woes; and I'm not merely talking about how it can help people with schizophrenia and depression and constipation. How many marriages, for example, would not even have happened if a man was not allowed to light a lady's cigarette for her?

Nicotine is a powerful, useful, albeit addictive substance desired by a great many people in a vast financial market. Who should have control of this wonder drug? Shouldn't it be the industry that literally spent centuries and countless dollars marketing it? In a capitalistic society such as ours, isn't the one who paid for it the rightful owner of it? So who has paid for and therefore owns the rights to nicotine? Let's take a look.

In 2011, the tobacco industry spent $8.37 billion on promotional expenses in the United States. Besides the usual magazine ads, distribution of free samples, payments to retailers for brand placement and direct-mail advertising, 83% of this money was used to give out price discounts to appease the lower class unemployed liberals. In the world of cigarettes, there are three companies that, when combined, control 85% of the market and they sell about 250 billion cigarettes in the United States every year.

So ask yourself: is it fair that an unregulated cottage industry with ties to China should infringe upon the rights of these giants who have spent trillions of dollars in their collective histories in order to supply the addictive drug of choice to the masses?

Also ask yourself what would happen if this trend continues, if at some point down the road there are no more cigarettes and instead everyone is inhaling concentrated nicotine vapor without all the traditional stuff found in the products that are produced by America's 10,000 tobacco growing farms.

I'm sure if you've made it this far into this book you are an intelligent person, so use your imagination to visualize what America will look like if cigarettes are banned and only vaping products are allowed. Can you really imagine tapping the guy next to you at a party and asking him for a battery charger rather than a match? Or having homeless people on the street bumming a drip instead of a square?

I'm sure you are visualizing this odd Daliesque version of our future where garbage men are unemployed because there are no more cigarette butts and you are laughing at how preposterous it sounds, but you should know it *could* happen.

This is why the smokers of the world need to unite and stand up against the ever expanding vaping industry, before we can no longer enjoy the manly, rich flavor of toasted tobacco and we will need to resort to huffing vanilla cream pudding instead.

Stand Up and Fight for Smokers' Rights,

Morrison L. Drall, Chairman,
Institute for the Preservation
of the Institution of Cigarettes

MEVLIN PROVARIO IS BACK.
WITH A VENGEANCE!!

Comiing Soon

ANGEL OF VAPE

Only from Vaporacle